T0129220

"I think everybody agrees with the significance of the male role model in society and in the family unit. Anything that helps to strengthen families helps to strengthen the wider community.

Rob Garrett is one of the many great men in our church. He serves as a dedicated Christian volunteer and is highly regarded by staff members and guest ministry alike.

Writing a book about parenting and fatherhood is a large task and requires personal experience and great grasp of the topic.

It won't take you very many pages to realise that Rob has been part of an amazing legacy, has a great biblical understanding and writes in a way that gives all of us hope for a better future.

This book is easy to read and is filled with many personal stories from other fathers to show how to put these ideas into practice.

My prayer is that you would be inspired to take the next steps necessary to become all God desires for you in parenting and fatherhood."

—Joel A'Bell
Lead Pastor, Hillsong Church Australia

"I recall my conversation with Robert about the men's response when I asked the conference delegates 'who would say they don't want to be like their father?'

Robert's comments about why he hadn't lifted his hand that day were as inspiring to me as those that did. Something happened in Robert's heart over that weekend and this book is the result of that.

This book is a celebration of all who instead of saying like me '**I Am Not My Father**', want to say I am my fathers biggest fan.

Well done Robert and may many be blessed and helped through this great book."

—Paul Scanlon
International Leadership & Communication coach

"Here is an easy to read and helpful book which is full of interesting stories from the author and others about their positive experiences of having a good Dad. These stories include practical principles to aid you in your quest to be the best parent you can be.

If you don't like reading parenting from an academic perspective but want to maximise your effectiveness as a Dad this is the book for you."

—Neville Cox
Chairman, Focus on the Family Australia

"Unfortunately my experience of a father is vastly different from the very positive one outlined by Robert and expressed in this book. I suspect that there are many of you who would identify with my experience or worse.

That is why I highly recommend Robert's book, in which, through a combination of practical wisdom, spiritual insights and the personal testimony of himself and others he has created a great resource of healthy fatherhood, and you will be encouraged that poor experiences and dysfunctional examples do not have to be the pattern for years and generations to come.

Read it, engage with it and you could be the beginning of a whole new cycle of healthy and Godly fatherhood."

—Dr Tim Hanna
CEO, Compassion Australia

"Robert's genuine commitment to men becoming the best dads they can be is evident within his book, 'More Like the Father'. He has taken great care in combining lived experiences of fatherhood, along with research, resources and biblical examples of the Father to guide the reader on the journey of Fatherhood.

Within his book, Robert shares his own experiences and learnings of being a son and a father to encourage other men on their adventure of fatherhood. With his deep respect for the experiences of others, Robert has had other men share how their own experiences with their fathers have impacted their role of being a dad.

Together with these lived experiences, and with reference to the Bible, Robert encourages the reader to consider a range of attributes and values central to being a healthy parent and father. He offers practical steps to the reader on how to consider their role or potential role of being a father, as well as highlighting that fatherhood is done with others – our families and with those around us.

Well done Robert on having the courage to share your story, so that others have the opportunity to learn from a genuinely lived experience of fatherhood."

—Dr Rebecca Loundar
Clinical and Counselling Psychologist MAPS

MORE LIKE THE FATHER

WISDOM FROM SONS OF GREAT FATHERS

ROBERT GARRETT

WESTBOW
PRESS®
A DIVISION OF THOMAS NELSON
& ZONDERVAN

WestBow Press books may be ordered through booksellers or by contacting:

WestBow Press
A Division of Thomas Nelson & Zondervan
1663 Liberty Drive
Bloomington, IN 47403
www.westbowpress.com
1 (866) 928-1240

Because of the dynamic nature of the Internet, any web addresses or
links contained in this book may have changed since publication and
may no longer be valid. The views expressed in this work are solely those
of the author and do not necessarily reflect the views of the publisher,
and the publisher hereby disclaims any responsibility for them.

ISBN: 978-1-5127-9014-6 (sc)
ISBN: 978-1-5127-9015-3 (hc)
ISBN: 978-1-5127-9013-9 (e)

Library of Congress Control Number: 2017908604

Print information available on the last page.

WestBow Press rev. date: 7/31/2017

This book is dedicated to my Dad and my Grandad who have lived lives worth emulating. I am forever grateful for their example that has set me up to win as a husband and a father.

It is dedicated to the men from many different backgrounds whose stories you will read within these pages.
I admire their willingness to be vulnerable and share their personal stories. These stories bear testimony to the truth that regardless of your heritage or where you are now, change is possible and we can all make choices to become More Like The Father.

Introduction

I have a number of heroes in the faith—men and women who are changing the face of the contemporary church across the globe. One such hero is Pastor Paul Scanlon, founder of Abundant Life Church England, who is one of the great teachers and communicators of our generation.

Late in 2007, Paul was in Australia to speak at a Men's Conference. During that conference, Paul launched his incredibly powerful book *I am not my Father*[1].

The book is largely autobiographical as Paul tells the story of his own dysfunctional experience of being fathered, and how he left home at sixteen to get married. By the age of twenty, unhappy with life and married with three young children, Paul had an epiphany moment where he realised that history was repeating itself and he was becoming just like his father.

The book goes on to explain that the forces of generational momentum are so strongly stacked against us that unless we make a conscious effort to make a defiant stand and say, 'I am not my father', we are likely to repeat the mistakes of our fathers and their fathers before them.

After introducing his message, Paul asked the five thousand conference delegates: "Who, after considering how you were fathered, would say 'I am not my father?'" Somewhere between sixty to seventy percent of the men raised their hands, causing

Paul to remark, "It's incredible, that whenever I ask that question to groups of men all over the world, the response is always the same—there are never less than sixty percent of men who raise their hands."

I spoke with Paul after his session and expressed surprise at the number of men who responded to his question. At this, Paul was prompted to ask me about my fathering experience. I said that I was one of the forty percent who did not raise their hand. I went on to explain that my own father and grandfather were two of my greatest heroes; both loved God, loved their wives and have been wonderful role models for me.

After telling my story, Paul commented: "You need to understand that your experience is not normal—what you've just described is the exception."

With a few hours of free time until the evening session of the conference, I found a quiet corner in the courtyard of a small café, ordered a coffee and began to read Paul's book.

I have never read a book cover to cover in one sitting, but after two hours, I'd finished. I sat back reflecting on what I had just read. I thought to myself, 'If I grew up with a dysfunctional father and didn't want history to repeat itself, where would I go to learn what a good father looks like?'

It was then that I recalled something that Paul said in our conversation earlier that afternoon, "Maybe one day someone will write a book from the perspective of the forty percent."

I am not a person who often goes around saying, 'God spoke to me about...' but sitting in the café that afternoon I believe that God stirred something deep inside me. My 'exceptional' experience of fathering wasn't just for me. At least sixty percent of men, who didn't have a positive role model must be looking for some answers, some guidance on how to 'do fatherhood' better. I genuinely sensed that one day I would write a book from the perspective of the minority—the 'forty percenters'.

Over the years, I've met some truly great dads who stood out from the crowd—exceptional men whose sons and daughters have the deepest love and respect for them. I believe that one of the best indicators of a great father is when his son says that, for the most part, he would like to be more like his father. That's not to say that he wants to become a carbon copy. Even the men with the best fatherhood role models that I've spoken to are aware that there are at least a few of their dad's characteristics they wouldn't necessarily want to replicate.

In one sense, great dads wouldn't want their sons to become copies of them. They would want their sons to embrace the positive qualities, behaviours and mindsets, and then build on those as they become the unique person God created them to be. That's the benefit of creating positive generational momentum. To use a building analogy—as fathers, our ceiling becomes our sons' floor. They don't have to start at 'ground level'—they take the great things they have learned and keep building on that foundation.

But this book is not about the search for the perfect father, because I don't believe such a person exists this side of heaven. By including the stories of a number of men who have had great dads, we can start to draw a better picture of great fatherhood, based on their collection of experiences.

As I talked to these men and read their stories, I discovered that great fathers fall into one of two groups. Either they themselves had great fathers and they were simply following their father's positive example, or they had a poor, dysfunctional father experience and as a conscious act determined that the negative generational momentum stops with them.

The great news that you can take from these stories is that if you didn't have the best fatherhood role model, then your past doesn't have to determine your future. You can choose how your story ends. Having drawn a line in the sand, this book will help you to start taking positive steps towards becoming a great father to your children. My prayer is that the testimonies within these pages will inspire you and give you hope that positive generational change is possible.

The other lesson from the lives of these fathers is that their stand-out qualities are actually reflections of the nature of our Heavenly Father. If you are a Christian, that probably won't surprise you. The first chapter of the Bible records that, "God created mankind in his own image" (Gen.1:27). Just as the law of gravity affects us all whether we understand it or not, the principles in this book will work for all fathers irrespective of their level of faith or belief in God.

If you are a father, don't overwhelm yourself by trying to incorporate all the traits described in this book simultaneously. As you read, choose one or two at a time, incorporating them into your parenting habits, before introducing the next.

If you are a single mum with sons, look for good men within your world who display some of these characteristics. They might be a brother, your dad, an uncle, or a close family friend; find opportunities for your boys to spend time with these healthy role models.

If you are a young woman who hopes to marry and start a family some day, write a list of the things you are looking for in a man. Be sure to include plenty of the character traits and behaviours discussed in this book, not only because I say they are worthy traits to look out for, but because they describe the different characteristics of God, our Heavenly Father.

Reading through the account of creation in Genesis 1 I'm reminded of the importance of connection and involving others in our individual journeys. As God completed each part of creation—the waters, light, the stars, the creatures of the sea, the plants, the animals, He stepped back, surveyed His handy- work and declared 'that it was good'. The first time that we hear God declaring that something is 'not good' is Gen 2:18 when referring to man being alone. It's clear that we are meant to do life in community with others.

So, as you read this book, be sure to look after yourself. Some of the stories shared in these pages touch on a number of topics, which although symptomatic of the world in which we live, may trigger memories of past disappointments or hurts.

For some, talking the issue through with a family member, friend or mentor will be helpful. However, if you need more support, can I encourage you to seek counsel from your doctor or other health care professionals who can come alongside you on your journey.

1

Describing 'Normal'

The funny thing about 'normal' is that both the child who wakes up each day in the most opulent palace and the child who wakes up each day on a rubbish dump would probably describe their life as 'normal'.

With no other frames of reference, 'normal' describes those ordinary everyday occurrences that are commonplace in your world.

It is not until someone comes along and shows you another frame of reference that you might decide to improve or change your 'normal'. The amazing thing is that if we don't like those everyday occurrences or behaviours that we see, we can choose to change—that is what sets us apart as human beings from all other creatures.

Let me paint a picture of what my normal looked like. The second eldest (and only boy) of four children, I was born in middle class suburban Sydney, Australia. I had a mum and a dad who loved each other and two sets of grandparents who lived nearby. We lived in a nice suburb, went to a good school and, like many in our neighbourhood, we belonged to a local church. Looking at our family, there was nothing unusual about us, we were...normal.

When I was six, Mum became ill with Hodgkin's disease and two months after my seventh birthday she passed away, leaving behind four young children (eight, seven, three, and twenty months) and a husband in his early thirties.

In the months that followed, the four children spent most of the week shared between grandparents, going home on the weekends so that we could all be together. For eleven months, my father was both 'Super Dad' and 'Super Mum'. He had a full time job Monday to Friday and in the evening and at weekends he did everything he could to keep his family of five together, making sure we never went without.

In April the following year, Dad took a well-deserved break and went on a cruise to Fiji and it was on that cruise that he met Jan, who was to become my second mum. She was a single mother with two young children aged four and two.

Dad and Mum married in June 1973 and a few years later they had a child between them, so to borrow the title from the old film, our family literally comprised of *Yours, Mine & Ours.* Perhaps it was because my siblings and I were so young when our family was 'blended', but the 'S' word (step...) has never been part of our family's vocabulary.

While my father was clearly more than capable of doing any household chore, generally speaking, Dad and Mum assumed traditional roles. Being part of such a big family meant that everyone played a part in the running of the household.

It was very evident that Dad and Mum loved one another and enjoyed each other's company. They held hands and spoke fondly of one another. Like every married couple, they had disagreements, but for my parents these were very few and far between, not explosive, and were resolved quickly.

Looking back, I can see that they had a good balance of together and apart activities and interests. They were one of the few married couples I knew who spoke with a great deal of excitement and anticipation about retirement and spending *more* time with each other.

Now in retirement, and after more than forty years of

marriage, they are more in love than ever. The security that children feel knowing that their parents are very much in love and committed to one another cannot be overstated.

AMISH'S STORY

I only have positive memories of my childhood. Dad and Mum both worked shift work and alternated shifts to make sure someone was always at home to look after us. Family was a big priority to dad and he worked hard to give us everything we needed. He was the hardest person to buy for, as he never wanted anything. He spent everything on us.

Dad did not become a Christian until I was in my late teens, though always came to church with us to support mum and do things as a family. A major reason we are all in church today is due to dad agreeing to move to a bigger church that had kids our age. Dad was wise enough to realise we needed friends, especially coming into our teenage years (we moved churches when I was 12). To this day all his kids (and their families) are serving God in their local churches.

Our house was small, but many people came when we had prayer meetings and Bible studies. Others (some we had never met before) came to stay when they were visiting or migrating to Australia. It was not uncommon for our house to host another family in our three bedroom one bathroom house. Dad taught us that people were more important than things and therefore we learned to share what we had.

Dad always put family first. Now retired, both my parents travel extensively, though the main purpose of their travel is always to visit people (generally family who are spread all over the world).

Despite the busyness of life, Dad is still always available to pray with and for us and provide practical help when needed. Even though I have a family of my own, he is still my dad and I am still his son and he still treats me as such.

He is in regular contact to make sure we are okay. Both he and Mum consistently provide practical help—cooking meals and spending time with our kids, who call him 'Pa' and think he is very funny. He is 'hands-on' and wants to be involved in our day-to-day lives.

To this day, Dad and Mum spend the first part of their morning praying and doing their devotionals—putting God first. If I need prayer, he and mum are the first ones I turn to. If I need anything I know I can always turn to Dad. I have always said he would give me his right arm if I needed it.

My father is a great man. He lives God's word, loves my mum, his kids and extended family. He is generous, kind and always puts others first. I would be proud if someone told me I am like him.

2

Great fathers have non-negotiable principles

In the early years of my life, we belonged to a small Churches of Christ congregation in Sydney's Northern Beaches. My grandparents, who moved to the area when it was still considered rural Sydney, established the church. Consequently, many of my earliest memories are centred around church life.

The practice within the Churches of Christ was to share in the Lord's Supper (or Communion) in every Sunday service. At the conclusion of the service, my Grandad would take the unused elements from the Communion table to a small room out the back, wash the Communion glasses and put the wafer biscuits back in a container for next week.

One Sunday night when I was about five years old, my oldest sister and I followed Grandad out the back, as we often did. Perhaps the curiosity of watching hundreds of Communion services finally got the better of us when we decided to take advantage of an opportunity to drink one of the small glasses of grape juice when Grandad wasn't looking. Emboldened by our victory, we decided to pocket a few pieces of wafer biscuits for later.

Driving home from church that evening, quietly in the back seat my sister and I were covertly enjoying our spoils. I thought we were being discreet, but we soon discovered we weren't using the same degree of stealth we'd used earlier in stealing the wafers.

When we arrived home, Dad sat us down and asked whose idea it was to steal the Communion wafers. Our lack of discretion in concealing our 'crime' was well and truly exceeded by our ability to keep the details secret. We were like a vault. We sat on the end of the bed for what seemed like hours and despite numerous attempts, Dad failed to draw any information from us.

Dad remained calm throughout the 'interrogation', occasionally leaving the room to give us time to contemplate our sins. Eventually he returned announcing that if we didn't tell the truth, he would have no option but to send us away to the home for naughty children because he and Mum wouldn't have children who lie and steal in the house.

The threat of expulsion from the house did the trick—we quickly confessed, ushering in a time of repentance (albeit not without appropriate consequences the next day).

Now you may think that threatening a five and six year old with expulsion from the family home is a little drastic, but in hindsight, I admire my Dad for the firm position he took.

In essence, Dad was saying that a principle was at stake—a principle far too valuable to abandon just because two little tight-lipped kids were tired. To simply let this pass with a smack on the backside and a warning "don't do it again" would have watered down a fundamental principle that, 'In our house, we tell the truth'. It was a key life lesson that has since remained with me.

There are several instances in the Bible where our Heavenly Father took a similarly tough stance. In Exodus 32 we read how the Israelites made a golden calf in the desert and began to worship it, so God instructed the Levites to go through the camp and kill the 3,000 people involved. In 2 Samuel 6:6-7, God strikes Uzzah dead for steadying the Ark of the Covenant after the oxen pulling it stumbled on the road. Seems a bit tough on a guy who was just trying to protect the Ark!

The story of Ananias and Sapphira in Acts 5 seems equally tough. The background for their story is found in the previous chapter; the New Testament churches were in such close community they did not consider their possessions as their own. Their devotion to God was so great that some believers sold houses or land and gave the sale proceeds to the apostles who distributed to anyone who was in need. Ananias and Sapphira were part of this community. They too sold some property; however, they were a little creative with the truth, telling the apostles that they had given the full proceeds when in fact they had kept a little back for themselves. For that lie, they both lost their lives and shortly after they were buried we are told, "Great fear seized the whole church and all who heard about these events." (Acts 5:11)

Many times after reading these stories I would think, 'Wow God, isn't that a bit over the top?' Then one day I heard a preacher say that if you ever find yourself thinking that way, then somewhere in the story you'll find a principle or truth that is so important to God that He simply can't ignore it.

God is not just truthful; He *IS* Truth. Therefore, to have turned His back on Ananias and Sapphira's lie would set a dangerous precedent amongst His newly established church. Similarly, my father's tough stance on the Communion theft and cover up cemented two important lessons in our young lives—the importance of telling the truth and that the Lord's Supper is holy and of special significance to Christians, not an opportunity for a late night snack!

As a parent, what are those non-negotiables in your family? What are the truths or principles that you are going to uphold, no matter what? I hope that telling the truth is one of them, but consider some others such as:

- Respecting those in authority:
  "Everyone must submit himself to the governing authorities, for there is no authority except that which

God has established. The authorities that exist have been established by God." (Rom. 13:1)

- Honouring your father and mother:
  "Honour your father and your mother"—which is the first commandment with a promise—"that it may go well with you and that you may enjoy long life on the earth." (Eph. 6:2)

- Principle of the tithe:
  Jesus said, "You should tithe, yes, but do not neglect the more important things [giving to the poor, justice and loving God]." (Luke 11:42b NLT)

- Looking after orphans and widows:
  "Religion that God our Father accepts as pure and faultless is this: to look after orphans and widows in their distress and to keep oneself from being polluted by the world."(James 1:27)

Look for opportunities, particularly when your children are young, to teach these life lessons. God knew that telling the truth was a critical issue in His young, newly formed church and that going soft on this issue in the early years would be damaging to the church in the long term. Establishing those important lessons early in life will help set up your young child for a great future.

A few years ago, we sold a car and the purchaser asked me to record a lesser purchase price on the Notice of Sale papers than what he actually paid, so that he would pay a reduced amount of stamp duty to the government. Financially, it made no difference to me, however, I was not prepared to sign a piece of paper that did not reflect the truth.

Many would reason this away in their mind, that a little 'creative truth-telling' is okay "...because the government already has too much of my money". I'm sure Ananias and Sapphira reasoned away their actions in their minds, but we already know that didn't end well for them.

When our principles come with conditions or qualifiers, when our actions do not line up with the lessons we teach our children, they live in a world without clear boundaries. In effect we teach them to add 'if' clauses to the principles in God's Word. For example:

We tell the truth IF it doesn't get us into trouble.

We tithe IF there's money left over after paying our bills and living expenses.

We respect those in government IF they're from the political party for which we vote.

I thank God for a father who, early on, took the opportunity to powerfully instil in me some key life lessons. He made the boundaries clear and has continued to uncompromisingly live out those principles in his own life.

Key Points from this Chapter:

- When we read stories in the bible where it appears that God's reaction is extreme, we need to ask—what is the fundamental truth or principle that is so important to God that He simply can't look the other way or ignore it?
- What are those truths or principles that you are going to uphold in your family no matter what?
- Look for opportunities, particularly when your children are young to teach these life lessons.
- When our principles come with conditions, or our actions don't line up with the lessons we teach our children, they live in a world without clear boundaries.

Robert Garrett

BARRY'S STORY

Recently, I read a quote that said, "Childhood is that period of life when parents build the room of the temple, in which later God will dwell, when the child is an adult." My father was a builder by trade but with his words and the example of his life, he built the structure of my early life and that of my two older siblings.

Dad cared greatly for both the natural and spiritual needs of his family. One of my earliest memories was every weekend when Dad would gather all our family's shoes and polish them until they shone in preparation for Sunday School and 'big church'.

My father built my childhood home and though it was modest by today's standards, back then our neighbours considered it 'classy'. The iron railing across the front had the words *'Fair Haven'* wrought into it. This wording impacted all of us as children, and in later life, all our homes were called by this name.

Dad always demonstrated love by kissing us, right up until he went to be with Jesus at age 77. But Dad was no push over. You would *never* give my dad 'cheek'. He would dish out appropriate punishment very willingly where we deserved it (and I did!). My dad modelled the Father's love... "Whom the Lord loves, He chastens..." (Heb. 12:6 NKJV)

At *Fair Haven*, we had a small garden where Dad cultivated his roses, frangipani, daphne, poppies and pansies. But we children had a part to play in its care. On Saturdays, we often went to the local swimming pool, but before we went, we had to weed the garden. If it wasn't done well, we couldn't go to the pool. *Arrrgh!* Early in life, Dad taught us a good work ethic and to avoid the human tendency for 'instant gratification'.

When I was only five or six, Dad went away for about five months to build a mission station on the edge of the Gibson Desert in Western Australia. Much later in life, Dad and Mum went back as Superintendents of the mission. His actions taught us to live a life of a servant-leader.

My most memorable times with Dad were when we all moved

to a country town where Dad pioneered a church as a lay Pastor, coinciding with me starting High School. He loved the Word of God and at the dinner table, we regularly had family devotions. As it was a small church, I was in Dad's Bible class and I am forever grateful that he chose some of the pinnacle chapters of the Bible for us to learn by heart, such as Isaiah 53 and 1 Corinthians 13.

Although Dad was a busy man, he always made time for family. He was a keen fisherman and as teenagers, we would quite regularly travel to a secluded rock shelf on the South Coast of N.S.W. and camp overnight. He demonstrated so much patience when untangling my line—an all too regular occurrence!

I am so grateful that God used my Dad (and Mum) to pass on to our generation the virtues of Christ centred living.

DAVID'S STORY (BARRY'S SON)

Dad, you are my hero.

At 48 years old, I am the second eldest of four boys, born 4 years after Dad and Mum were married in 1963.

My Dad is strong...physically, mentally and spiritually. His Dad was the same. My lineage has strength, character and blessing, with the foundations laid by the men before us. Success is a part of all his son's lives because of the seeds Dad sowed and the example he poured into our lives as boys and young men. Dad taught me how to love God, love people, work hard, play hard, be fair, be humble, be courageous, be compassionate, be honourable, respect my elders and always without exception place God in the centre of all I do.

None of that is easy and commitment is always required. My father's example has always been there; Dad never takes a backward step in anything he does. I am sure he has been afraid and challenged plenty of times in his life, but I never saw it as a child. Even as I grew into manhood, I never witnessed fear stop him doing what he knew he needed to do. He was not reckless; but rather I would describe him as courageous and wise in his approach to any situation. I have felt fear many times in my life but Dad taught me to trust God and believe in my abilities for the very best result.

Because of my father's consistent example, I have always given 100% in everything. Even today, in his mid-seventies, Dad gives 100% in all he does. Whether helping a couple with broken hearts, pulling weeds in the vegie garden or painting a door, I know he puts everything into it. Occasionally, I would hear Dad makes comments like, "By the sweat of your brow" and "C'mon - let's get stuck into it!" But mostly it wasn't his words but his actions that made a difference to me. Words come easily but backing it up with actions is what really matters.

I have five children and as a Dad, I am now passing on the many things Dad taught me. Something all my children have heard me say occasionally is, "I can't hear what you say...I only see what you do".

My father's greatest quality and example to me is his ability to love people. He has shown me how to extend grace, compassion, patience and love to those around me. As I mellow and gain more years under my belt, I have learned to listen even more to my Dad and follow his lead on how to do life.

Dad has set the bar high but in hindsight, I wouldn't have it any other way. If I can at least be half the man my dad is, I will have done okay, but he continues to be an inspiration to me to give all I have in being the very best I can. I can hear his encouraging words now in my mind, saying, "Go for it Davo!"

I am proud of my Dad—he is my best mate.

3

Great fathers think generationally

When Dad remarried, our modest three-bedroom house was clearly too small for eight people. Shoehorned into the main bedroom were a bunk bed and two singles for my four sisters. My new brother and I shared a room while Dad and Mum squeezed their bed into the smallest bedroom.

Finding a new house was a priority. Three months after the wedding, we sold our house and moved across Sydney to a larger house. Our new home was about five minutes from my aunty and uncle's house, so my cousin invited me to go to Boys Brigade at his church. (Similar to Scouts, Boys Brigade is a Christian based program focusing on the physical, spiritual, educational and social development of boys.)

I enjoyed the structure and discipline of Boys Brigade. Before long, I invited the two boys who lived next door to join me. After a year or two, Dad decided to start a Boys Brigade group at our own church.

Now, if there was anyone who could have justified not taking on something like setting up and running a boys program it would have been my Dad, particularly as he and Mum had just had their seventh child! Nevertheless, he recognised a real need to reach, develop and mentor a generation of boys. If you had to choose a man from our church with the patience and godly character to pull off such a feat, someone whose guidance you would want your son to come under, then in my opinion, you couldn't find a better candidate than my dad.

It didn't take too long before we had thirty to forty boys meeting every week. A reasonable number of these boys, such as the two boys from next door, two boys from across the road and another from around the corner, were from families who were not connected with any church. A few times each year as part of the Sunday evening church service we had a parade and the boys' parents and siblings would often come along. For some, this was the only time they heard the Gospel message.

We went on numerous camping trips and some incredibly gruelling hikes. I remember the time we hiked through the Blue Mountains from Faulconbridge to Glenbrook. At the end of the first day of hiking, we set up camp and caught yabbies in the creek, cooking them for dinner. The next day the track we were following disappeared and with steep rocks either side of the creek, we walked down the centre of the creek holding our packs over our head because in some places the water was up to our chests. Those times were fun but they were also painful; they built qualities such as resilience, discipline, problem solving and perseverance into us.

We learned so many skills over the years in Boys Brigade, but most of all, we established some life-long friendships. There was a young man who had grown up in our church and was dating a girl from another church in the next suburb. He invited his girlfriend's younger brother to come along to Boys Brigade. That brother became one of my closest friends and went on to marry my second eldest sister.

As I'm writing this chapter, one of the younger Brigade boys comes to mind—an adopted boy with a reputation at school and in his neighbourhood as a bit of an uncontrollable troublemaker. In all the years he was in Boys Brigade, I don't recall ever seeing his father. His dad never dropped him off or picked him up, never came to the end-of-year award nights.

Curious to see what might have become of him some 35 years later, I suspended the writing of this chapter to Google search his name. Surveying the results, I happened to find an article about him in a rural newspaper. The story told how he was searching for and finally connected with his birth mother. He is now happily married with a few children and talked about how great his in-laws are. After learning a trade, he is now running his own business and employing a few locals as apprentices. By the looks of things, he has turned things around and made a real success of his life.

I am not saying that the influence of Boys Brigade was the pivotal factor in turning around his life; however, I am confident that the impact of those seeds which were sown into his young, troubled life played a significant role.

There is no doubt that my dad could have found any number of far less stressful ways to occupy himself that wouldn't have required hours of preparation each week for the Friday night program. Instead, he chose to make a valuable investment into my generation. Had it not been for Friday nights at Brigade some of those boys would never have heard the Gospel. Some of them had tough or absent dads, while for others, Friday nights were possibly the only time they had an adult male authority figure affirm them.

Dad's decision to invest into the next generation is not common. In his book *The Battle for the Loins*[2], about the power of generational momentum, Paul Scanlon writes, "western societies do not automatically think in genealogies or generations like God does. Our attitude to life is characterised more by maxims such as 'seize the day!' We tend to think just about ourselves, we 'take care of number one' and concentrate only on the things we can do in our lifetime rather than giving much thought to those who will come after us."

While western society may not think generationally, we know that God does. We read in Hebrews 7 where the Old Testament character Levi (father of the Israelite tribe of the Levites) paid a tithe to the High Priest Melchizedek. It's a curious story because Levi and Melchizedek weren't alive at the same time.

In order to understand how God thinks generationally, we look in Exodus 3, where God introduces himself to Moses at the burning bush. He says that He is the God of Abraham, the God of Isaac and the God of Jacob—three successive generations, and this is the first time He introduces Himself this way. Levi is in fact one of Jacob's 12 sons and therefore Abraham is Levi's great grandfather.

Hebrews 7:10 explains that, "Because when Melchizedek met Abraham, Levi was still in the body of his ancestor [Abraham]." In other words, Levi's seed, genetically speaking, was in Abraham, and as Paul (Scanlon) explains, "Even though Levi was nearly a hundred years downstream of Abraham chronologically speaking, as far as God was concerned the actions of Abraham had a direct effect on his unborn offspring."

So if we think as God thinks about the people within the people, who knows how many people have been—and are yet to be—impacted by those six years that my dad invested in the development of that group of boys?

In a very practical sense, through his involvement with Boys Brigade, Dad made a way: for his future son-in-law to enter our lives, for my sister to find her life partner and subsequently for their three yet-to-be-born children.

As dads, are we thinking generationally or just living for the here and now? Do we think about the long-term consequences of the decisions we're making today and the scores of people who will be impacted by those decisions?

We need to be looking for opportunities to build into the generations that are coming after us. What does that look like for you? Perhaps it's coaching your child's sports team or helping to lead the youth program in your church. Perhaps it's taking one of your son's mates who doesn't have a father under your wing and being a positive role model in his life.

My wife and I are passionate about building strong, healthy Christian marriages. For more than ten years we've been taking young engaged couples through a program called Prepare. (Prepare is a questionnaire-based, facilitated discussion that explores a couple's relationship strengths and growth areas and aims to provide the foundations on which to build a great marriage.)

In that time, we have probably worked with over thirty couples—it's something we love to do, but sometimes it's a sacrifice: running in the door after a long day at work and gulping down dinner; putting our three children into bed in the fifteen minute window before the couple arrive at our house; spending time studying their questionnaire responses and planning the appropriate questions to ask; creating an environment for the couple to safely discuss their different experiences, approaches and values that they will bring to their marriage relationship.

To be honest there are some nights when I think, 'I'm just not in the mood for this', and I'm sure there were times when Dad thought the same way about Boys Brigade. But are we just thinking about ourselves or are we thinking about those who will come after us? It is conceivable that one of the couples we have taken through the Prepare program could have a child that one day becomes our son or daughter-in-law; when we approach it with that mindset, the investment of our time takes on a whole new perspective.

Great fathers look beyond themselves and think generationally.

Key Points from this Chapter:

- God thinks generationally and looks at the yet-to-be-born lives within a person.

- Who knows how many lives generationally downstream from us will be impacted by the decisions we make today?
- Living with a generational mindset sometimes means that there are sacrifices to be made in the present for the good of future generations.

DAVID'S STORY (This is my Dad)

When I think about my father and how his values and example influenced my life, it is not difficult to say that I would definitely like to be more like him. In fact, when I think back, I believe I have unconsciously modelled my life as a Christian father, husband and citizen on the example he set for me in all these areas.

Although I never knew my paternal grandfather, I do know that he was an alcoholic and not a good role model whatsoever. Despite this, my father was able to rise above his negative influence to set his sights on what he believed a good father should be—something I really admire about him.

Throughout my early years, my father spent much of his life as a Sergeant in the Australian Army, having served in both WW1 and WW2. I did not see a lot of him until I was about eight or nine years of age when he was discharged and resumed life as a normal working civilian.

We lived in Frenchs Forest on a small acreage farming poultry, fruit and vegetables; Dad was always doing something of a practical nature. Although he had no qualifications in a trade or profession, he was able to put his hand to almost anything from building to agriculture or mechanics. Working alongside him enabled me to gain a solid grounding that prepared me for my adult life. My chosen trade as a motor engineer was greatly influenced from my working alongside my Dad on our 1928 model A Ford. There was nothing on that car that Dad could not tackle and his ingenuity in approaching various repairs had an enormous influence on me.

My Dad had a tremendous love for my Mum and there was nothing he would not do for her that was within his financial or practical ability. They went through many hard times together including one stillborn child and the loss of another through accidental drowning. Their financial status was never strong but their faith in God was—one area where I would like to be more like him. Dad declared his faith in Jesus during his early twenties and has always been a strong witness to his faith. He was the prime mover in starting two new churches, resurrecting another and serving on a number of church committees. He demonstrated fervent support of Social Services and Aboriginal Missions, always thinking of the welfare of others.

I would never describe my father as an avid follower of any particular competitive sport. However, he was supportive of enjoying a game of cricket or football as a means of fun, exercise, developing co-ordination and team effort. During his fifties, he started a 'Young Explorers' club for young boys where these skills were taught along with practical life skills and spiritual values, giving them a kick-start into life beyond public education. It has only struck me recently that I have followed in a similar vein when training as a 'Boys Brigade' Captain and resurrecting the 'Boys Brigade' Company in our local church. These same values were passed onto the boys in our Company and I have had the privilege to see many of them become successful carpenters, electricians, doctors, motor mechanics, bankers, teachers, solicitors and managers.

My Dad was a man of prayer and action. He lived out the words of James 2:18 where he states, "Show me your faith without deeds, and I will show you my faith by what I do." (NIV) My prayer has always been that through my example I've been able to pass on the values and life lessons I learned from my Dad to our children, setting them up for success as they parent their own children. As a parent, as a father, there is no greater sense of satisfaction or humility in life than to watch that transfer from one generation to the next.

4

Great fathers take responsibility

At 33 years of age, I was single, had a nice car, a good job, and had just purchased my first house. I had travelled to some parts of Australia that most Australian's haven't seen and spent a month exploring New Zealand driving from top to bottom.

I still remember a day back in 1996 when one of my friends remarked, "Wouldn't it be fun to visit Hong Kong before it's handed back to the Chinese?" My other friends and I quickly agreed and the next thing I knew, we had booked a holiday to Hong Kong, Macau and southern China. A few years later, some other friends suggested a visit to South Africa and Zimbabwe. While on the African continent, I took the opportunity to spend some time in Egypt and then catch up with some other friends for a few days in Singapore on the way home.

This is not one of those 'who has the most stamps in their passport?' conversations; I'm just trying to paint a picture of a carefree lifestyle with very little responsibility and contrast that to my Dad at the same age.

In contrast, when my dad was thirty-three, my mother passed away and he instantly became a single parent with four children aged between twenty months and eight years. Many decades later Dad said that if it hadn't been for the wonderful help from his mother and mother-in-law, he would have unquestionably caved in and given up.

Every week while Dad was at work, my elder sister and I stayed with Dad's parents, as they lived close to our school. My two younger sisters stayed with Mum's parents who lived a little further away. At the end of the week, Dad would pick us up from our grandparents'. For the weekend, we were all together again. Over the next twelve months that process repeated each week. Dad remembers this as the loneliest time of his entire life.

Nine months later, Dad met a young woman—also a single parent, whose husband left for another woman. Almost twelve months after we had lost Mum, dad had remarried. I had a new mother and we all moved back home permanently.

Divorce can be messy. As a young boy, I remember Mum's ex-husband coming to our house every few weekends to take my new brother and sister out for the day as part of the custody arrangement. As he walked down the driveway and mum met him at the front door, we held our breath, knowing what was coming next. There would often be an exchange between them at the doorstep, over maintenance payments. Then as he drove away in his Mercedes, Mum would come back in the house and that was our cue to make ourselves scarce for a while.

In his podcast series *Taking Responsibility for Your Life*[3], Pastor Andy Stanley says that when a person refuses to take responsibility for his or her actions, their irresponsibility ultimately becomes someone else's responsibility.

It is an all too common scenario on television or the movies played out in real life that when a person who is self-medicating by overindulging in alcohol, food or drugs is confronted, they respond by saying that they're not hurting anyone else. In effect, they are saying, 'Hey what's it to you? I'm an island, sure this might not be good for me, but I'm only doing it to myself so mind your own business and leave me alone.'

But that's not true. The truth is that we live in a connected world and we are connected to one another in some way. Consider the person living on their own with no family or friends, who is irresponsible with their health. Eventually this person will end up in hospital, and taxpayers ultimately take responsibility as their taxes fund the medical system. If the issue is financial irresponsibility, the interest rates and bank fees that we all pay factor in a portion to cover a certain number of accounts or loans the banks statistically know will inevitably become bad debts.

This ripple effect of irresponsibility can be seen in the Old Testament book of Joshua chapter 7. The Israelites have just witnessed the city of Jericho fall after they marched around it seven times and made a lot of noise. God's instruction to them was very clear—burn everything in the city; anything made of precious metal was to be put in the treasury of God's house.

Fresh from their victory at Jericho, a few Israelites go to spy out the next obstacle—a town called Ai. They report to Joshua that the town of Ai should be a walk in the park after Jericho and suggest that there is no need to send the entire Israelite army— perhaps two or three thousand men should be sufficient—the rest can have the day off. On their advice, Joshua only sends three thousand men. The Israelite army is defeated losing thirty-six soldiers in battle, and nobody—especially Joshua—can figure out what went wrong.

Joshua starts blaming God for bringing them across the Jordan River and while he's praying and crying out, God speaks to him and says, "Get up! Why are you lying on your face like this? Israel has stolen some of the things that I commanded must be set apart for me. And they have not only stolen them but have lied about it and hidden the things among their own belongings. That is why the Israelites are running from their enemies in defeat." (Josh. 7:10-12 NLT)

To cut a long story short, Joshua goes through the Israelite camp and sure enough, some guy called Achan has kept some robes, silver coins and a gold bar for himself, burying them under his tent. For his disobedience and irresponsibility, Achan and all his family were stoned to death and their bodies burned. Disaster was averted and God's favour returned. Israel returned and defeated Ai and burned the city to the ground.

What I find particularly interesting about this story is that in verse 11 God says to Joshua that <u>Israel</u> has stolen some things. If I were a lawyer witnessing this conversation between God and Joshua (and with the benefit of knowing how the story ends), I'd interject at this point and say, "Objection God—the nation of Israel has done no such thing. I don't want to mention names, but if you were to go on a bit of a treasure hunt around the camp (hint: maybe look under the corner of a few tents) you'll find that only <u>one</u> person has been irresponsible by disobeying God and keeping some of the plunder."

God is all knowing, so His purpose in holding the whole nation of Israel responsible wasn't so that He could find the real culprit. This is another of those Ananias and Sapphira stories mentioned earlier where we need to stop and think—if God allowed Achan and his whole family to be stoned to death and then burned, then there must be a really important issue going on here. God knew that Achan was the thief; therefore His comment gives us an important insight into how God sees His people. We do not live in a vacuum; what we do affects those around us.

If we were to put Achan in the witness box he would probably say something like—"What's it to you? I just kept a few things. No one would have missed them. I wasn't hurting anyone."

In fact, Achan does eventually take responsibility for his actions and, to his credit, he doesn't try to implicate or blame anyone else, "...I wanted them so much that I took them. They are hidden in the ground beneath my tent..." (Josh. 7:21 NLT). But it was too late; thirty-six of his fellow soldiers were dead and if we think about the knock-on effect in terms of immediate family and friends, the number of people directly impacted by this one man's decision would have been in the hundreds, possibly thousands.

Our Heavenly Father shows us how to take responsibility. The basic premise of the gospel story is that of God taking responsibility for our irresponsibility. Throughout history, mankind has exercised free will, making choices that have separated us from God; however, God the Father did not simply shrug His shoulders and give up on humanity. When He sent His only son Jesus to become the once-and-for-all sin sacrifice, He took responsibility and made a way to restore personal relationship between humanity and Himself—our Creator.

If you are a father, then you have responsibilities. There are people in your world who are counting on you, people who are impacted by the decisions you make. Even if you are not a dad, but hope to be one day, the decisions you are making today will affect others. Popular thinking may argue that your single days are for wild irresponsible living, and that marriage and family life is for settling down and being responsible, but that is not the truth.

Too many men discover later in life that the choices they made in their single, supposedly 'carefree days' impact both themselves and their family later on in life. Lifestyle choices have the potential to affect physical, financial and mental health. For example, it's difficult to travel or enjoy retirement if you are waiting for a liver transplant as a result of young adult years of wild partying.

I deeply admire the fact that my Dad took responsibility for his own children after we lost Mum; but he also took responsibility for another man's irresponsibility, not just financially, but in providing a secure, loving family home for his newest two children. What I find even more remarkable is that I have never heard my father say a bad word about Mum's ex-husband or complain that he wasn't taking financial responsibility for his children.

Great fathers take responsibility.

Key Points from this Chapter:

- Nobody is an island—other people are always impacted by the decisions we make.
- The actions of one man—Achan in the Old Testament—affected an entire nation.
- When a person refuses to take responsibility for his or her actions, their irresponsibility ultimately becomes someone else's responsibility.
- If you are a father you have responsibilities; there are people in your world who are counting on you.
- God the Father took responsibility for bridging the gap between Himself and mankind by sending His only son Jesus.

MARK'S STORY

I grew up in a home that was a real safe haven—a home where my two brothers and I found love, provision and protection. A decade after my youngest brother was born, my parents had a little girl. She really was the apple of Dad's eye and still is. But my parents never had 'favourites', investing equally and sacrificially into all our lives.

Dad was a shift worker and mum stayed home and loved us with an unconditional commitment to our well-being. As a young boy, I presumed that everyone enjoyed the same loving, safe home environment that we had.

It probably wasn't until my high school years that I began to see how many others were living in circumstances in such contrast to what we experienced, and I realised just how blessed we were.

Although I could speak at length about my mother's significant investment into our lives, this story is about my dad. My dad's father was an atheist and a very antagonistic man. I think that my dad is the most amazing man for breaking away from the patterns that were modelled to him by our grandfather and creating a brand new heritage for our family.

To begin with, he gave up the alcohol and cigarettes that finally brought on the strokes that killed both his parents. Next, he demonstrated what was important by how he invested his time. Unlike his dad, he was at everything we were involved in. Looking back it must have been difficult for him to change his shifts around to be more involved in our lives, but he was completely committed to his family.

For example, when we joined the Scouts, he trained to become a Scout leader. When we attended the local church youth group, he volunteered to be a youth leader.

My siblings and I now all have children of our own, and to this day, Dad remains committed to being involved in each of our lives. He is helping one brother with his cars, another brother with his house, my sister with her renovations and me in my ministry life.

From a generational perspective, breaking away from the destructive patterns of his father and building a life of faith, paved the way for me to meet Jesus Christ at an early age, and for that, I can never thank him enough.

Even though Dad could have excused church attendance because of a busy life with four kids and shift work, he made sure we were there every week. He continues to model a life of integrity, Christian service and personal devotion to God. The reason Dad is such a blessing to others is that he is a very practical example of what it means to live out the godly qualities of love, joy, peace, patience, kindness and so on. I have been a very grateful recipient of the overflow and outworking of this in his life.

I have spent more than twenty years pastoring and so much of what I do has come from the foundation my father laid, breaking away from the patterns of his own father and introducing me to my Heavenly Father. I know my dad is proud of me and loves me. I believe it is because of this that I relate to my Heavenly Father as a loving, providing and safe God who is always for me and always disciplines me toward being a finer man.

Now, with three boys of my own, I seek to be so much like my dad as I invest in them. Recently I was humbled when all of my teenage boys wrote beautiful letters affirming me as a father and a role model. All I can say is thank you Dad—you have started the most amazing legacy.

5

Great fathers go the extra mile

Growing up in a family of nine, I think our lifestyle would be best described as frugal; there was nothing extravagant about the way we lived. For most of our formative years, our family 'car' was a big, bright red, ex-Qantas Airways Ford Transit van with twelve seats. Family holidays were usually spent camping in a tent at a caravan park about forty minutes from home on Sydney's Northern Beaches, and our grandmother often knitted our school jumpers (imagine the teasing we endured in the school playground).

It was rare to have a tradesman of any kind doing work at our house. Dad was an automotive engineer and has always been very practical with his hands. Whether working with wood, metal, plumbing or electrical work, he did it all. Only a few years ago when Dad was in his early seventies, he built a two-storey granny flat on their property at the foot of the Blue Mountains.

When appliances broke, he pulled them apart and fixed them. Not only did he fix our things, it was not uncommon for friends and relatives to drop off lawn mowers and other items that needed repairing.

Repairing engines was dad's speciality—I don't recall any of our cars ever going to a mechanic to be serviced, he did it all himself—not only our own cars, but our friends' cars as well.

I remember the girl in our church who was the youth group leader for many years. One time, she asked Dad for some mechanical advice, and after diagnosing the problem, he offered to carry out the repairs...

So, one long-weekend, she dropped her green Mini at our house for Dad to work on it while she was away. The repairs didn't take long, so Dad gave the whole car a general check over. Generally, the Mini was in good condition, but the paintwork had seen better days.

Dad spent the remainder of the weekend working well into the night, rubbing back all the paintwork, repairing a few minor parking indiscretions and repainting the whole car.

Needless to say that when the owner came back to collect her car there were squeals, hugs, and happy tears.

Too often there's a bare minimum mindset that pervades our culture—how much do I *have* to do? What is the least amount of effort that I can get away with?

When Jesus walked on earth, He introduced a very different way of thinking. In Matthew 5:41 He talked about going the extra mile. What does that look like in a practical sense? Dad could have diagnosed the mechanical problem with the Mini and given a referral to a good mechanic. Our youth leader would have been better off than if she had to drive around to find someone who could identify the problem and then get a few quotes to have the work done. Instead, he went the extra mile, offering to fix the car himself for just the price of the necessary parts.

However, he didn't stop there, he actually went the extra-extra mile and returned the car looking almost as good as when it left the showroom.

A few years ago, a good friend of ours installed a remote control gate on our driveway. When I arrived home from work, he was just finishing up. My friend spent time stepping me through the installation and how to use the remotes. But he then showed me how, rather than only connecting the power to the motor on the gate, he'd figured that because he had to bring electricity to the far end of our house, he had installed a double power point in case we wanted to access electricity at that end of the yard.

Then he made an extra-mile statement, "It's always been my philosophy on every job I do to leave the client with a little surprise—something extra that they weren't expecting."

How often do we role model 'just enough' fatherhood to our children?

As I am writing this, I'm reminded of one of those moments that happened only a few weeks ago. It was almost the end of the soccer season for our two boys and my wife Cath was telling me that my youngest son's team was rostered on for the barbeque and the canteen at their home ground in two weeks time.

Firstly a little context—we didn't grow up with weekend sport in our family (imagine trying to get seven kids to seven different games!), so if I'm honest, I don't always wake up on Saturday morning with the best attitude towards the kids' sport. Secondly, both our boys had their respective soccer matches at different times that Saturday morning and at different locations. After their matches we would have to race home, have lunch and then go out again and cook sausage and bacon and egg sandwiches for the people at the matches for the older teams in the club.

My first question to Cath was—what time are we rostered on? My second question revealed my 'minimal requirements' mindset—what time do we finish? In other words, what's the *least* amount I *have* to do?

In his sermon on the mount in Matthew 5, Jesus introduces the idea of going the extra mile. The NIV Bible subtitles the section from verse 38-42 "Eye for Eye", and although the context is how we should respond to those who seek to do us wrong, how much more should this generous approach to life apply to those we care for? I love The Message translation of verse 40, "If someone drags you into court and sues the shirt from off your back, gift wrap your best coat and make a present of it."

Where would we be today if Jesus had role-modelled a 'just enough' mindset when he came to earth? I'm trying to imagine how that conversation might have sounded in heaven...

God tells His son Jesus that the only way to reconcile a broken humanity is by giving a perfect sacrifice once, and for all. "Oh, and by the way, you're it! Did I mention you will need to go to earth be born in a barn, grow up in humble surroundings, be misunderstood and written off by your neighbours as just 'the carpenter's kid'? You will lead a team of twelve men (they're a bit of a motley crew) but their support for you will be hot and cold. Your own people will love you one minute and want to kill you the next. You'll be whipped and beaten to within an inch of your life, and then they will actually crucify you on a cross."

Imagine if Jesus had responded, "Look, I can deal with the bit about the barn and being misunderstood. But crucifixion? Couldn't I just put a bit of extra effort in with the twelve guys and send them out to convince the world of how much You love them? Once they're up and running, I could quietly return to heaven and leave them to it."

Thankfully, our Heavenly Father is the God of the extra-extra-extra mile. He created us and according to James 1:18 (NLT), we are God's prized possession out of all creation. Yet, although humanity turned its back on Him time and time again, He pursued us and devised a plan to reconcile us by the giving of His very best in order that we can be restored to a right relationship with Him.

Great fathers go the extra mile. If your children asked you to climb up to get the tarpaulin off the top shelf in the garage so they can make a tent, would you just stop what you're doing long enough to comply? Or would you also find a few other items around the garage that could be useful—a ladder, a piece of rope, a few poles?

Would you check back in with them in twenty or thirty minutes to see if they need a little engineering expertise to hold up the roof of the tent? Would you show genuine interest by asking them to call you when the tent is finished, so that you can check out their creation and have a pretend sleepover?

As earthly fathers, one of our key responsibilities is to set up our children with a healthy view of fathering. Too many people struggle with their understanding of God as their Heavenly Father because their only frame of reference is their earthly father, and all too often, that has not been a particularly good experience.

I don't want to do anything that would cause my children to have a negative concept of a father. It is my hope that their relationship with their Heavenly Father would build upon a positive foundation modelled from their earthly father.

One of the many names of God recorded in the Bible is *El Shaddai*, which means *One who abundantly blesses with all manner of blessings*. How can our children relate to their Heavenly Father in this way if their earthly father only ever demonstrated minimal requirements, who only did 'just enough'?

Be a dad who goes the extra mile. When we go above and beyond our children's expectations, those are the times they will remember well into their adult years.

Great fathers look for the opportunity to go the extra mile and model a life of generosity.

Key Points from this Chapter:

- Too often there's a bare minimum mindset that pervades our culture, but Jesus taught us to go the extra mile.
- Our children will struggle to understand the 'exceedingly abundantly above all that we ask or think' nature of God the Father (Eph. 3:20 NKJV) if we've role modelled 'minimal requirements' fatherhood.
- Thankfully, Jesus didn't have a minimum requirements mindset when it came to our salvation.

ANDREW'S STORY

Dad was married to my mum for forty-nine years and I am one of four of his children. My earliest and latest memories of him are nothing but positive. Dad worked in the public service for over forty years and volunteered for over thirty years at our church, using and developing his gift of hospitality. Our family benefited greatly by Dad using this gift to show his love and affection for us all, wherever and in whatever way he could.

My Dad had many qualities that I admired and will always remember. One of these was that he was always present physically and emotionally. As a seven year old, I remember how Dad regularly drove me to sport on Saturday mornings, cheering me on and always encouraging me. He always seemed to be there at our highest and lowest moments. We had many great holidays as a family, both local and overseas. Dad's greatest enjoyment was not the sightseeing but being with us wherever we were.

One of his greatest strengths was acts of service. Dad made many sacrifices on many occasions to show us his kindness whether we were well behaved or not. From the moment our family woke up, Dad had already been in each of our rooms to place a hot-chocolate or coffee at our bedside before he left for work; he did this for me until I left home. When my wife and I came to visit, he would prepare us some food at short notice and without fail, he would always walk us to our car and stand at the driveway waving goodbye, regardless of the time or weather. We did not ask or expect it - to be honest, there were many times we used to tell him to not do so much, yet to my amazement, as he aged he seemed to excel even more in this area.

It was very rare for my dad to talk about his needs and wants. He was not self-centred, neither did he expect life to revolve around him. His needs and wants were what God wanted and this was his attitude right until he went to be with the Lord. If he had to go without, he would quite happily do so without any fuss. My father's generosity came without any conditions—there were never expectations, obligations or any kind of strings attached.

Just like Barnabas in the Bible, Dad was a fantastic encourager. I have heard many reports from people who knew my father through our church and abroad—phone calls to say hello, cards sent to uplift someone's spirit, saving seats for people running late to church and conferences. He would consistently leave spontaneous notes and cards of encouragement for me, or messages on my phone that drew on Scripture. I could not begin to count how many times he laid his hands on me praying for my protection, favour and blessing.

My Dad made a deliberate effort to teach me many life skills; he often did this in a very practical way by involving me in things that he was doing. We grew up in the country and he taught me how to grow all sorts of vegetables and fruits in our garden, while caring and raising animals (sheep, budgerigars, turkeys and breeding chickens to name a few)—these are still wonderful memories for me.

My Dad loved God's Word, the Church and prayer. Sneaking home after a late night university party at 3:00am, many times I observed him in the kitchen reading his Bible and praying. He was waiting up and praying. I realise now that my Dad possibly knew that some things just needed prayer.

Dad had an energy for life that few his age have. Blessed with great health, every week he ushered and hosted at our church until he was 85 (very few knew his true age). He always had time to visit people at home or hospital, while still finding the time for each of us, including his grandchildren. One of Dad's greatest joys was to spend time with my two boys— he was never too busy or tired for a visit. He just loved to help and be around people.

I don't think I ever took my father's approach to life and love for granted. Especially now as a dad myself, I have learned that modelling Christ's love to my wife and children produces a great foundation for the next generation, as well as a great sense of security that is so critical today.

I have never doubted my dad's love, which made me appreciate him even more later in life. Instead of him initiating contact, I wanted to contact him and see how he was going. I think this was a great joy for him, knowing that his son wanted to spend time with him. He was a very simple, uncomplicated person whom God used to be a profound father to me.

The message of God's grace on Dad's life is that he never had a father figure, and when he was ten years old, his mother passed away. Despite being placed in homes and being raised in different Christian orphanages, he knew that God was always with him.

Whenever I think of my dad, my response will always be, 'Thank You Lord.'

6
Great fathers make time

In many cultures, family mealtime is about more than the simple physiology of putting fuel in our tanks. It's been said that food and mealtimes are the social 'glue' that reinforce relationships and bring groups of people closer together. Yet we live in an age when employers demand more and more of their people, and this can mean early starts and late finishes, putting pressure on family mealtimes at either end of the day.

Growing up in our house, Dad always made mealtimes a priority; occasionally he would leave home early to fly interstate, but it was very rare that he wasn't home for both breakfast and dinner throughout the week.

Even when a new role or promotion put greater demand on his time, he would make sure he was home for dinner and then do some paperwork after dinner if necessary.

Mealtimes involved everyone sitting around the meal table—not sitting in the lounge room in front of the television and definitely no television humming away in the background. Meals were a time for family conversation, to talk about the day's events and nobody left the table at the end of the meal until everyone had finished eating. This was no 'drop-in diner'; this is where connection happened.

Even now—some twenty to thirty years since my siblings and

I left home—a number of our collective memories are centered around events and conversations that took place at the meal table. For example, the times when I would try to make my younger siblings laugh to get them in trouble when Mum and Dad left the table and went into the kitchen—what a great big brother!

Years ago, I was a senior manager with one of the top twenty banks in the world. At the turn of the millennium, we had purchased another Global Top 100 company and I was part of a small team focusing on the cultural integration of two very large companies.

Organisational culture is often misunderstood and there can be a significant gap between the culture, as described by the CEO or the leadership team, and that which is experienced every day by employees and even their customers.

To help us navigate the complexities, we engaged a woman who was a renowned expert on organisational culture. Before we could even start to develop a cultural integration plan, it was critical that we first had a clear picture of the culture in each organisation. This would highlight any similarities and differences in the two cultures and would start to quantify the gap that would form the basis of our work over the coming years.

Our culture expert taught me a simple truth that I've never forgotten—she said that you can easily determine an organisation's values—those things on which they place great importance—by how they prioritise their limited resources: time and money. For example, an organisation that says that people are its most important resource yet only spends 0.05% of profit on training and development sends a clear message that profitability is more important than people.

What is true for corporations is also true for individuals. If you want to find out what is important to a person, have a look at their diary and bank statements. Time and money are limited resources; each of us have only 24 hours in a day. Even billionaires have to make decisions on how they spend or invest their money, and those choices will reveal the things that are most important to them.

An article in The Guardian in June 2014[4] referenced research undertaken by Dr Almudena Sevilla of the School of Business at the University of London and Cristina Borra of the University of Seville, which showed that in 2014 the average working father spent 35 minutes per day with his children. While at first this figure might seem a little on the low side, it's considerably higher than the 5 minutes per day recorded 40 years earlier in 1974. The research concluded that fathers were finding the additional time from their working lives as they had a greater appreciation of the importance of fatherhood versus career.

Credit where credit is due dads, that's a seven-fold increase, but it's still a fair way behind the results for mothers for the same time periods – 15 minutes per day in 1974 versus one hour a day in 2014.

So how do we find more time to spend with our children? As we've already established, we find time for those things in our lives that we think are important. Which activities are currently taking priority in your life? Can they be re-prioritised or can you re-order your diary so that family time isn't pushed into the 'only if there's enough time left over' category?

A few years ago, I started a consulting business. When you are a sole operator, there can be wild peaks and troughs in your workload. Some months it's a 'feast' working 16 hours a day, six days a week, whilst other months it's 'famine' more like two or three days a week. To be honest, since we started, the ratio of feast to famine has been about 90:10.

My biggest client has been one of the giants of the telecommunications sector. When it comes to flexible work practices, they 'walk the talk' more than any organisation I've worked with (or for). Flexibility can mean different things to different people and one day the project team I was working with sat down to have a discussion about what flexibility meant for each of us.

One person said that she'd like to work from home one day per week and that would generally be on a Wednesday. She added that she could swap days if there was an important team meeting on a Wednesday. Another person shared that he didn't like sitting in peak hour traffic; he preferred to log in from his laptop from home at around 8am, clear his emails and then arrive at the office around 9:30/10:00am. At the other end of the day, he would typically leave mid afternoon, do a gym session on the way home and log back in around 4pm for a few more hours.

When it was my turn, I said that my family are my absolute highest priority. Unless I had to travel interstate or had a critical early or late meeting, my goal was to be home for at least one mealtime at either end of the day, preferably both. If I had to be in for a 7am meeting, expect me to be gone around 4:30pm to be home in time for dinner; if there was an after work function, I would probably take the kids to school after breakfast before coming in to the office. I added that on a typical day, I hoped to have left the office by 5:00pm in order to be home for dinner with the family and that I was happy to log back in at home and continue working after the children had gone to bed.

By the time everyone had shared, the team had a very clear understanding of what flexibility meant to each person, including their priorities and boundaries. In other words, these things are negotiable if circumstances require it, but these other things are not.

Let's be honest, those conversations aren't that common, but that's beginning to change. There was a recent article in Australia's number one business newspaper quoting the CEO of a very large corporation saying that the approach to flexible working arrangements had to change. He said that it was unacceptable that he'd missed his children's birthdays, school events and even the birth of some of his children.

There is a growing acceptance of the need for more of these conversations to happen, particularly as the ratio of Gen Y and Gen Z employees in the workplace increases. One of the hallmarks of these two young generations is that they aren't prepared to sell their soul to an organisation (like their parents did) because they know that the company isn't going to be loyal to them when it's looking to reduce operating expenses. So they're looking for a more matrix style of employment arrangement, where work is incorporated in and around other roles, responsibilities and interests.

The hands-on, day-to-day influence that we have with our children lasts for such a relatively short amount of time. Do whatever it takes to maximise the time that you have with them; be bold and start the conversation in your workplace about flexibility, boundaries and priorities.

As a dad, I feel blessed that our children want to spend time with me. "Come kick the soccer ball with us", "Let's play cricket", "Can we please read together?", "Come watch this dance I just made up", "Can you take us on a bike ride to the BMX track?" The requests can come thick and fast, so how do we fit them all in? The reality is that we can't always, and the more children you have, the greater the challenge. Imagine if my dad had accepted every request from all seven of his children.

We shouldn't just equate quality time with our children to accepting invitations in to their world. A key lesson that I learned from my own father was that as dads we can invite our children into our world; quality time doesn't always have to be about Lego, computer games, Barbie dolls and Disney movies.

Mowing the lawn during an Australian summer is often a weekly occurrence; miss a week or two and you could be sending out a search party to find the kids in the backyard. Saturday afternoon was usually the time for mowing at our house. Dad had an old Victa lawn mower; it was very basic—a dark green metal plate of steel with a wheel at each corner, an engine sitting on top and a tubular metal handle. There was no grass catcher at the back, so the mower simply cut the grass and flung it in every direction across the yard.

Before I was old enough to go to school, I recall that as soon as the engine on the mower had stopped, we were enlisted to rake up all the grass clippings. The rake handle was more than twice as tall as I was, but I still had a go. After a while, Dad would take over and rake the grass clippings into small piles around the yard. Our job was to collect the piles of grass in the wheelbarrow. Once we were finished and the yard was tidy, we climbed into the wheelbarrow and Dad took us for a ride, running like a crazy man around the yard. It was memorable, quality time spent together; it was us getting involved in Dad's world. He didn't have to choose between necessary chores and time with the kids.

Dad spent a good portion of his working life employed by our state's motoring association; later in his career his role was to road-test new vehicles and write reviews for the members' monthly motoring magazine. This meant that he was always bringing home new cars. From my early teens, I could tell by the sound of the car coming down the driveway whether it was something other than his regular company car. Before he could stop the car, I'd be standing at the driver's door waiting for him to get out, so that I could jump in and check it out. About fifteen minutes later—after testing the seats, playing with the stereo and everything that opened and shut—I would come into the house, toss Dad the keys and give him my thoughts.

There were several times when I took a day off school (or a rostered day off work when I was older) to join Dad on one of his detailed road-tests. On one such occasion, he'd brought home a black V8 Ford Mustang convertible. Our routine was to leave home in the morning while it was still dark and drive to a racetrack on the other side of Sydney. For the first few hours of the day he had the racetrack to himself, and with all manner of computer equipment strapped to the car, he'd test acceleration, brakes, cornering etc.

Mid-morning we left the racetrack and headed north along a variety of roads—straight, winding, dirt and tar. Around mid-afternoon, we would end up at the New South Wales Central Coast before heading back to Sydney on the freeway. They were long and tiring days, but the best memories I have are of that one-on-one time with my Dad, where he invited me into his world. When would he have been able to carve out ten straight hours of his day to spend with me otherwise?

This is a practice that I've carried on with my own children. It's not quite as exciting as going to a racetrack with a Mustang or a supercharged Jaguar, but one day in each school holidays one of them comes to work with me. The bus ride is often a highlight, particularly driving over the Sydney Harbour Bridge and past the Opera House (things I take for granted on my daily commute).

During the school holidays it's usually a little quieter in the office so we find a space where they can watch a few movies on the laptop and do some colouring in. I stop work to have morning and afternoon tea with them and they choose where we go for lunch.

Recently we were having a clean up in the boy's bedroom and we were trying to throw out things that they'd outgrown or no longer played with. One of these is a small ceramic snow leopard that had been given to our youngest son by a colleague. I picked up the leopard and holding it over the rubbish bin said to him, "You don't need to keep this do you? You never play with it."

"No way," he said, "I'm keeping that because it reminds me of the day I came to work with you." He then went on to recall in great detail the events of the day—the bus trip, the movies he watched, the kind lady who gave him the leopard, and what we ate for lunch.

Never underestimate how big a deal it is for a child to be invited into their dad's world. Not only is it an opportunity for some quality time together, it also helps them to uncover the mystery about what dad does in those hours between leaving the house after breakfast and returning home in the evening.

We are all busy, but great fathers make time, both to be involved in their children's worlds and to invite their children into theirs.

Key Points from this Chapter:

- The easiest way to identify what we value the most is to identify where we spend our time and our money.
- Spending quality time with your children doesn't always have to be about Lego, slot cars, Barbie dolls and Disney movies. Look for opportunities to invite your children into your world.
- Inviting your children into your world gives them insight into what you do between leaving the house in the morning and returning at the end of each day.
- The hands-on, day-to-day influence that we have over our children lasts for a relatively short amount of time. Do whatever it takes to maximise the time that you have with them.
- Start a conversation at work about what working flexibly and life balance means to each person in your team. It's healthy to understand your colleagues' boundaries concerning their time, and which things are negotiable under certain circumstances.

DAVID C'S STORY

It's funny how becoming a husband and a father provides perspective on what our parents did for us when we were children.

My Dad has always been a busy man; he had a career in senior executive roles for one of the biggest financial institutions in our country. As part of his role, he was chairman of 26 companies. Outside of work he was involved in leadership roles for churches and various ministries, playing music, crisis counselling, mentoring and president of the school P&C...basically anything his three children were a part of.

Both my parents have a very strong work ethic, yet when we were growing up they made sure that they were present during our 'awake' hours, fitting in other commitments while we were sleeping or at school. Many of my friends' dads were absent fathers even though they didn't seem to have as demanding jobs so I was interested to talk to Dad in recent years about how he balanced work, life and ministry.

I discovered that there was plenty of work, travel and time away; however, he worked very hard to be home at the dinner table and present for our big sport matches or music recitals. Where possible, Dad would hold meetings at our house so that he wasn't always going out. As part of his job he often had to face the media and he would arrange for them to meet us after my soccer game at an agreed location.

Dad taught me how to do many things, was patient with me when I wanted to do the painting, the paving or fixing something. He passed on the skills and sayings that his father had shared with him. One of those key life lessons was to "Get down to the level of the job." This isn't just literally about getting down on the ground when painting the bottom of the fence, but rather about being prepared to get down to the right level with life, in my attitude, my humility and with others.

As a kid, I remember playing soccer and it was my turn to be goalie. I didn't want to play that position because I didn't want to let my team down. But my dad was right there with me standing behind the nets. He wasn't thinking about his next board meeting or newspaper interview; he brought himself to my level, to what was going on in my world. Despite the tears streaming down my face he kept speaking to me, encouraging me and preparing me for the next ball and together we made it through the game.

Years later I was wrestling with life as a teenager. Like a lot of teenagers I knew it all and the relationship between my Dad and I had become fractured. As a result, I left home for several months which really hurt my family. One day the world I had built up fell down completely, I had nothing and nowhere to go. I asked Dad if we could meet and we went walking together. I told Dad that I had been a fool; I'll never forget how he wrapped his arms around me and welcomed me home. Looking back, I regret what I did but as a result, Dad and I learned something important about how to communicate, a better way of really listening to one another.

Now I'm a husband to a strong and courageous wife, and a Dad to five precious children. I'm learning for myself that raising kids is not easy; it requires a lot of patience. I am now using the life lessons and fathering skills that my parents taught us as kids. By God's grace, I run a business and I'm often called upon to demonstrate father figure traits to a broken world. But each day I come home, disconnect from my work role, ready to connect with my wife and to get down on the level with my children, sometimes literally getting down on the floor to play with them.

I'm sure I will make my fair share of mistakes, however I know the best I can give my kids is my time, to pray with them and to let them see me love and honour my wife.

Today, Dad is still busy serving, mentoring and releasing people to achieve their potential and I'm still busy watching and learning all I can from him. Our shared faith in Jesus unites us, and I love having the opportunity to worship with him and support his ministry endeavours as he continues to demonstrate incredible leadership in our country to unite all believers.

7
Great fathers are consistent

I recently watched a television documentary[5] about a wealthy American family. The dad was going through a difficult time financially and risked losing a significant chunk of his business empire. One evening he was bunkered down in his study, sitting on the lounge in front of a huge TV and surrounded by disorganized, towering piles of paperwork. His wife took his dinner to him on a tray. Her attempts to connect with him emotionally were unsuccessful and even her request for a little kiss before she left the room met with a cold refusal and a mini lecture about leaving lights on in the house.

The wife quietly tiptoed out of the study and as she shut the door she said to the cameraman (who filmed the whole awkward exchange from across the hall through the partially opened study door) that her husband is, "...not in a good mood tonight."

A few minutes later she returned with their son, who looked to be around ten years old. Her 'brief' to him before sending him in to the study was that daddy was in a bad mood tonight and what he really needed was to hear that his son loved him.

The son shuffled into the study, his dad barely averting his eyes from the television. After a few moments of small talk, he awkwardly told his dad that he loved him and as the son was leaving the study, he too received the lecture about leaving all the lights on in the house. The dad added that maybe he shouldn't pay the electricity bill so the house is without power; that way the whole family might learn to respect the cost of things.

The whole scenario of a family walking around on eggshells, trying to placate a grumpy old man was quite sad. Using one of their children (who already looked to have a distant relationship with his dad) as a pawn to try to make dad happy was heartbreaking.

One of the things I remember when growing up is that my dad was not prone to erratic mood swings. Like everyone else, I'm sure there were times when he had a bad day at work or when he was slightly overwhelmed by the pressures of managing the household budget for a family of nine, but he certainly didn't show it.

As evidenced in that documentary, a father can easily influence the emotional temperature of an entire household.

If you are a dad, how does your behaviour influence your household? Does your family look like an Olympic rowing team gliding effortlessly across a glass-smooth lake or more as though they're holding on for dear life on a jet ski—ripping across the glassy lake one day and launching off three-metre waves in the surf the next?

When I was in my early twenties, our church denomination ran an annual youth camp over the Easter weekend. One particular year, as was often the case, there was a group of forty to fifty young people from our church. One afternoon, we had a block of free time. Rather than participate in any of the optional organized activities, a group of my friends (including a few of my siblings) and I piled into three cars and decided to go 'exploring' in the nearby bush.

To make a long story short, the cars became separated and then we literally ran in to each other on the bend of a narrow dirt track. Thankfully, everyone was OK, but we had three badly damaged cars. Luckily, they were all driveable, so we returned to the campsite, parking the cars at the back of the car park hoping nobody would see them.

Bad news travels fast and before long most of the camp were talking about the accident. Red-faced with embarrassment, we had to explain ourselves to our youth pastor and then, one-by-one we were taken into a small room with a telephone, to call our parents.

When I called home, Mum answered. In that split second, I ran an imaginary conversation through my mind, "Hi Mum, its Robert. We're having a great time at youth camp. Just thought I should let you know that four of your children were involved in a three-car pile-up today. It would have been totally avoidable—if we'd remained at the campsite instead of hooning around the bush. Anyway, we are all OK, my car's not. See you when we get home on Monday, bye!"

So how did the conversation *really* go? Well, the first four words were the same, "Hi Mum, its Robert. Um... could I please speak to Dad?"

My Dad is a good listener and I knew that I'd get a calm response. He listened while I explained the necessary detail, occasionally punctuating the conversation with a calm word or two to let me know he was still there, "Oh! ... Really? ... Oh dear, is everyone OK? ... Probably not how you envisaged the weekend... Glad you're all OK - see you Monday."

If I'm honest, my actions that day probably warranted a stronger response, but I'm ever so grateful that Dad didn't add to how bad I was already feeling. He was the perfect example of James' encouragement, "Understand this, my dear brothers and sisters: You must all be quick to listen, slow to speak, and slow to get angry. Human anger doesn't produce the righteousness God desires." (James 1:19-20 NLT)

It's this same consistency that our Heavenly Father speaks of when describing himself, "I am the LORD, **I do not change...**" (Mal. 3:6a).

James also tells us that, "Whatever is good and perfect is a gift coming down to us from God our father, who created all the lights in the heavens. **He never changes or casts a shifting shadow**" (James 1:17 NLT).

The writer of Hebrews describes Jesus as "...**the same yesterday, today and forever**." (Heb. 13:8 NLT)

Imagine if every time we approached God in prayer we had to take a chance on how He was feeling that day. Will He be angry with me? Will He give me the strong silent treatment? Or will He show me love, grace and compassion? The very reason that we are encouraged to enter boldly into the throne room of grace (Hebrews 4:16) is because of the sacrifice of His son Jesus—once and for all; we no longer have to approach God through a mediator (or priest) as in the Old Testament. We know that when we approach Him we'll find love, acceptance and grace.

Just as the consistency of God's character brings security to our relationship with our Heavenly Father, when we are consistent fathers, our children will feel secure. This is particularly important in a world that is constantly changing.

Those things in society that previous generations looked upon as consistent, stable pillars—such as the economy and government—are no longer a certainty in the 21st Century. As an example of the inconsistencies with which we live, our nation has seen five prime ministers in five years. So even if I support a particular political party whose values align with mine, that party might hold its own internal ballot to replace our Prime Minister with another member of the party who may very well hold a different view on key issues such as the economy, climate change, marriage and family.

Today's children live with more uncertainty and change than any generation before them. When sailors are out in turbulent seas, they fix their eyes on the one constant—the horizon—to ward off seasickness. As a dad, I don't want to add to my children's uncertainty. I want to be one of the constants—the horizon they look to as a means of helping them cope with change.

When they come home from a party where their peers were

pressuring them to do something they didn't want to do, I want them to feel safe to share that with me, knowing that I won't lose my temper in a fit of rage and forbid them from going to all future parties until they're fifty. I want to demonstrate years of consistency where they know they can talk about such things with me and I'll calmly coach them towards making the right decision for themselves.

Very few parents set out to intentionally have a full-blown, explosive, relationship-destroying argument with their children at these major decision points in life. Becoming a consistent pillar of support starts with putting some 'consistency credits' in your children's emotional bank accounts when they are young.

In addition to emotional and behavioural consistency, consistency with our words is incredibly important. My wife and I have instructed our children from a very young age to, "Say what you mean and mean what you say." Sometimes when they're playing with one another I'll overhear them say something like, "If you let me... you can ride my new bike whenever you want." I remind them to be a person of their word and make sure they mean what they say.

On a number of occasions the kids have pulled us up for not delivering on something we said. Maybe we promised to take them to the park to play and for whatever reason it didn't eventuate. Of course we can usually explain our actions—if I didn't have to get the ladder out and retrieve your ball from the roof, if Nanna hadn't called for a chat, if Nat hadn't dropped by to return that DVD and stayed for a cuppa... if, if, if. The reasons could be many and legitimate, but the result for our kids is the same.

Depending on the child, they may verbalise their disappointment at the time or store it away for a later time. Others may quietly internalise it as they build a case in their head for why dad's word cannot be trusted.

Our youngest son decided to explore the game of cricket so we signed him up to junior cricket for a season to learn some basic skills. One Saturday morning the coach was running the boys through their warm-up exercises—running around the oval, star jumps and push ups etc. One of the boys decided that he didn't want to join the team exercises, preferring to wait for the batting and bowling to start.

The coach made several attempts to have him join in with the rest of the team, making it quite clear that if he didn't, he wouldn't be participating once they moved on to the other activities. To the coach's credit, he kept to his word; when the team moved on, he refused to be manipulated by the boy's tears and selfish behaviour.

Initially the boy's father stepped in, reiterating the coach's conditions, that once he'd completed all the warm-up exercises he could join in with the team. The more defiant the boy was, the angrier the father became toward the child, even threatening to take the boy home. I lost count of the father's threats after fifteen. Finally, the drama came to a head when he physically picked up his eight-year-old son and took him to his mother, who was quietly reading the newspaper on the sideline. The father said that he would stay at the oval with their younger son (who was also on the team) and instructed his wife to take the recalcitrant child home.

No sooner had the mother taken hold of her son's hand than he pulled away sharply and easily outran his father. Without saying a single word, she shrugged her shoulders, rolled her eyes and went back to her newspaper. After a few more idle threats, and perhaps sensing defeat, the father laid out three rubber traffic cones in a triangle about five metres apart and told his son that if he ran around those, he could join in with the rest of the team. This whole sorry incident finally concluded after about forty minutes.

Subliminally the boy would have taken away the following key messages:

- The coach says what he means and means what he says.
- My dad makes lots of idle threats and doesn't follow through.

- If I hold out long enough I can get my own way.
- Dad doesn't respect authority because he changed the coach's conditions for me to re-join the team.
- My parents don't back one another up when it comes to discipline.
- At eight years old, I can outrun my dad!

Build a consistent pattern, whereby your words line up with your actions. If you're not prepared to follow through with the threatened consequences, it's better not to make the threat in the first place. Jesus tells us in Matthew chapter 5 that we are to be people of our word—let your 'yes' mean 'yes' and your 'no' mean 'no'. In other words, say what you mean and mean what you say.

Great dads bring stability to their parenting and to the home, when they are consistent in their behaviours and emotions and have a proven track record for being a person of their word. Their children know where the boundaries lie, and that there are consequences if they choose to cross those boundaries.

Key Points from this Chapter:

- Consistency in how we behave and lead at home brings great stability for our children and household generally.
- When disciplining, avoid making idle threats; say what you mean and mean what you say.
- Let's be men of our word. Our children should know that dad's word can be trusted.
- Be one of the constants that your children look to, to help them navigate an ever-changing world.

DARYL'S STORY

My father was born into a strong, Christian heritage. His father was actively involved in the Methodist Church and his grandfather was a preacher.

Dad grew up on a property outside a small South Australian farming town that consisted of a church, a school, a blacksmith and a post office. Unable to work on the family farm because of his severe hay fever, he took a job as an apprentice motor mechanic, requiring he make his own way to and from work on his bicycle—a thirty kilometre round trip each day in the harsh extremes of the Australian climate.

Dad married, and following the completion of his apprenticeship (topping his class), he moved to Adelaide to pursue a job with General Motors Holden as a Service Adviser. My parent's ultimate desire was to become overseas missionaries. To this end, Dad spent a year studying in the evenings at Bible school, however when he applied for a missions role he was told that he was too young to be accepted. To his credit, Dad didn't let his disappointment affect his faith.

During my parent's time in Adelaide, my older brother was born. Dad soon realised that time with his young family was compromised by the constant need to travel for his work. Because family was first priority, he changed jobs and they moved back to the country. That's where I was born, followed by the birth of my younger, twin brothers. Dad continued to be a faithful employee and although his boss was grooming him for bigger things, God's plans were over and above what Dad could have imagined.

God graciously provided for us when Dad was given the opportunity to buy a country Ford dealership. Dad has always modelled a life of service to others. In this small country town, Dad sold cars and involved himself in the community by serving on the school council, as superintendent of the Sunday school and chairman of the hospital board. Those years studying at missions school were anything but wasted because in this new community,

Dad was given the opportunity to regularly preach as a lay preacher in the surrounding districts.

There have been times in my life when God has spoken to me about my future and I couldn't see how my job at the time was taking me toward that future. However I've learned from Dad's story that sometimes it's only with the benefit of hindsight that we can see the fruit from 'seeds' planted in faith.

Dad has always been strong and consistent in his parenting. On the mantelpiece in our home was a sign that read 'Christ is the Head of Our Home' and so being in church every Sunday (morning and evening service) was not negotiable. Church always took priority over sporting events because Dad knew that in those formative years we would learn key lessons—building blocks that would set us up for life.

Dad generally has very definite ideas about the way that things are to be done. As the middle child, I was often testing the boundaries and enjoyed looking for alternate ways to achieve the desired outcome. Early on this caused some friction between Dad and I, but as we've grown older I think he's come to appreciate that there can be different paths to the same destination. It's a valuable lesson that's influenced how I parent as I've learned to give my children a goal and then the freedom to find their own path to achieving it.

I have learned so much by observing my Dad as he modelled a life of faith and consistency. I've learned to hold onto what is right, even when things are falling down around me or when things aren't going as planned. From both Mum and Dad's example, I have learned the value of being in strong partnership, and I've been blessed to do parenthood with an amazing and strong woman by my side. The most important lesson I've learned is not to let anything steal my faith.

My wife and I have endeavoured to lay the same building blocks in our home with our children. Consistently building God's House is our priority; it's part of who we are. That commitment guides the decisions that we make, and when we're not sure of the way ahead we have the added advantage of the Holy Spirit who speaks wisdom into our situation. Our faith encourages us to stand on the foundation of God's Word, that immovable security that comes from being planted in Christ.

Our children are all adults now and are doing life well. It blesses me to see how the wisdom and the lessons that my father taught me are now bearing fruit in their lives as the next generation. We love spending quality time with them. And when we do, my wife and I have this sense that with God's help, we've done our best to set them up for their journey in life. Now it is their time to create their own adventure.

8

Great fathers show grace

It was a Sunday evening in the spring of 1993. I'd been out to supper with some of my friends after church and as I opened the front door at home and stepped into our living room, I realised something was seriously wrong. Dad, Mum, and about half of my siblings were sitting around on the lounges, but the room was strangely quiet. With a family the size of ours, the only time the house is quiet is when everyone is asleep or there's nobody home, so something was obviously amiss.

I can't recall whether it was Dad or Mum who spoke first. "Rob, your little sister has something to tell you."

It was then that I noticed that my sister's boyfriend was sitting next to her and that he wasn't making eye contact. My seventeen-year-old sister looked up at me and said, "Um, I'm pregnant; we're having a baby."

Raising my eyebrows and rolling my eyes to broadcast my disapproval, I turned and left the room without saying a word. A little while later, Dad came to find me. "Right now your little sister needs to hear from you, to know that you still love her" but I had no intention of doing anything of the sort. I was content to let her and her boyfriend feel the weight of my disappointment.

Walking back through the living room while avoiding eye contact with anyone, I mumbled a general "good night" and went to bed. However, I didn't sleep much though; the sound of Mum crying throughout the night in the room next to mine was heartbreaking.

The next day I woke up angry. With no thought for how my sister was feeling, I was furious at what she was putting my parents through—the two most important people in my world. Then came the final blow—Mum and Dad invited my sister's boyfriend to move in to our house once the baby was born. What were they thinking? How could they offer this after everything they'd been subjected to?

My response to my parents extending grace? "If he's moving in, I'm moving out."

Scouring the classifieds for a place to rent, I soon found a garden flat at the back of a big old house and moved out as quickly as I could. I thought my anger was justified, but looking back I'm ashamed at my self-righteousness.

In John chapter 8 we read how the teachers of the law and the Pharisees brought a woman who was caught in the act of adultery to Jesus, saying that according to the Law of Moses, she was condemned to be stoned.

This is the same Jesus who I, at the age of eight, had accepted as my personal Saviour—the same Jesus I had chosen to follow and model my life upon. What was His response? He invited those of her accusers who were without sin to throw the first stone and one by one, they dropped their rocks and quietly walked away.

When they had all gone, only Jesus and the woman remained. He looked around and asked her, "Where are your accusers? Didn't even one of them condemn you?" "No, Lord" she said. And Jesus said, "Neither do I. Go and sin no more." (John 8:10-11 NLT)

If anyone could have taken a morally righteous position it was Jesus, yet He didn't judge or condemn her. He didn't just show this woman grace, He IS grace personified. He came to earth as the freely given, unmerited, undeserved favour and love of God.

In contrast to my position of taking the moral high ground, my parents—the very ones I felt had been aggrieved—extended grace, and in doing so kept relationship with my sister and their (now) son-in-law. In a very practical sense, they provided a stable home environment for their new grandson to be born into.

I guess my own father's amazing display of grace was the perfect reflection of our Heavenly Father. The Old Testament is full of stories about God's children making choices that weren't in their best interests, and yet He continued to pursue them and ultimately made provision for reconciliation, by giving His son Jesus, to restore relationship.

As earthly fathers, how do we model grace to our children? If we don't provide opportunities to teach our children about grace and extend it to them in a very practical sense, they will struggle to comprehend how their Heavenly Father could love them and forgive them when they mess up. If we shut them out emotionally and make them earn their way back into our favour, we're teaching them that their father's love can be earned. The Bible calls this 'works' and if this is the type of fathering that we're modelling then our children will struggle with one of the most pivotal verses in Scripture, "God saved you **by his grace** when you believed. And **you can't take credit** for this; it is a **gift from God**. Salvation **is not a reward** for the good things we have done, so none of us can boast about it." (Eph. 2:8-9 NLT, emphasis added)

The essence of these two verses is that we've all messed up and made bad choices that would otherwise separate us from God. God saved us from the judgement that we deserve and the consequences of our choices—eternal separation from Him. However, if our being 'saved' were something we could earn by doing lots of good things, then the focus would be on us and how good we are rather than on Him and how great His love is towards us.

Indeed it's this 'come as you are, you don't have to do anything to earn it' message that sets the Christian faith apart from all other religions. If our children are familiar with receiving love and forgiveness from their earthly fathers (even when at times it may seem undeserved) how much more readily will they receive this same grace from their Heavenly Father.

I'm certainly not suggesting that we never let our children feel the consequences of their poor choices, or shield them from taking responsibility for their actions. Nevertheless, I do think that as fathers we need to find examples where we can practically demonstrate grace to our children. My suggestion is that if you're looking for opportunities to show grace, use an example where your child is clearly in the wrong and they know it. The whole point of grace is that we don't deserve it; so if they're not convinced that they're in the wrong, your demonstration of grace could easily be misconstrued as 'justice' – *Dad let me off, which is what I deserved anyway.*

When I've done this with my own children, I ask them what they believe the punishment should be. A repentant child who knows they're in the wrong will most likely be tough on themselves when choosing a punishment. This makes it all the sweeter when you step in and show them grace by not giving them the punishment they deserve.

Next, make sure that they understand why they are receiving grace. In our house, the conversation generally goes something like this,

"That was a terrible thing to do to your brother; what do you think the punishment should be?"

The child responds, "Perhaps no computer games and no television for the next two weeks."

"Okay, that sounds like an appropriate punishment. However the next two weeks is the school holidays and we've planned for our friends to come over for a few movie nights, so I'm choosing to show you grace—do you know what that means? "

"No not really."

"Grace is something that God gives to us; He chose to save us so we can spend eternity with Him even though we mess up and deserve punishment. Now I'm going to give YOU grace and will let you be involved in the movie nights when our friends come over."

That child now has a basic understanding of grace. Hopefully they won't draw back from God later in life because poor choices have them feeling unworthy. Having experienced grace from their earthly father over a smaller issue, they can receive grace from their Heavenly Father on weightier issues.

In Luke 7, Jesus is a dinner guest at Simon the Pharisee's house when a woman comes in to wash Jesus' feet with her tears, wipe them dry with her hair and pour perfume over them. His host is thinking, 'if this Jesus really is a prophet he'd know how sinful this woman is, and he wouldn't let her touch him.'

Perceiving what was in Simon's heart, Jesus tells a story about two people who owed money to a moneylender—one a small amount, the other a large amount. Jesus says that neither of them had the money to repay the lender so he cancelled both their debts. To drive his point home he asks Simon which of the borrowers would love the lender the most. Simon answers correctly that the one who has the most debt owing would be the most grateful and love the lender the most.

Dads—our children will no doubt give us plenty of opportunity to show them grace. By teaching them about God's grace towards us and practically demonstrating how that looks when they mess up, we not only help them to develop a healthy understanding of the heart of their heavenly Father, but our children will love us more—for the one who is forgiven much, loves much.

Great fathers show grace.

Key Points from this Chapter:

- As earthly fathers, we need to model grace to our children.
- If we don't provide opportunities to teach our children about grace and extend it to them in a very practical sense, they will struggle to comprehend how their heavenly Father could love them and forgive them when they mess up.
- If we emotionally shut our kids out and make them earn their way back into our favour when they mess up, we're teaching them that their father's love can be earned. The Bible calls this 'works' and is the opposite of grace.
- Repentant children will most likely be tough on themselves when choosing a punishment. This makes it all the sweeter when you step in to show them grace, by not giving them the punishment they deserve.

JACOB'S STORY

At only 23 years of age and the third of four children, I can't give as fully a matured testament to the good work of my father as others perhaps can about theirs. However, so far, I can say with certainty that I want to become more like him!

In light of this, it's interesting that if my Dad was asked the question, "Do you want to become more like your father?" his response would be a decided, "No." Dad was born and raised in a Christian household, although he didn't have a close relationship with his father. Due to his father's insecurities, the relationship between them was distant. He wasn't a rogue but I believe he struggled to show his true feelings towards my dad although this slowly mellowed as he got older and their relationship improved over time. Because of my Dad's experience, he made a deliberate decision to break that generational distance between father and son when he had his own children.

I believe that through those considered and deliberate choices my dad made not to become a repeat of his father, I gained a rich inheritance—a close and loving dad. I have many fond memories of quality time spent with him right through my childhood to today.

When I became old enough to drive and had passed my test, for my first car I became obsessed with the idea of getting an old vehicle. I preferred the classics, thinking they had a lot more character. So I trawled the Internet until I found "The Car!"—a 1977 Mk2 Escort. My dad was away working at the time and advised I should wait until he got back so that he could come and check it out with me. So, being the young, dutiful and obedient young son, of course I paid no attention to his advice and went ahead and purchased the car.

Here in the UK we have a little problem with old cars called RUST! To make a long story short, we soon found out my new purchase was an absolute 'rust bucket' underneath. But instead of abandoning me with my mess, Dad rolled up his sleeves and helped me carry out restoration work on the car!

I love the fact that I can always comfortably approach Dad with any subject or problem and rely on his wise advice, free from condemnation. Three years ago, about two weeks before my wife and I were to be married, we got a little carried away and broke our promise of purity to each other out of wedlock. We were so distraught and it was a really difficult time for us both. I'll never forget my parents' godly response of compassion and love when we sat in front of them sobbing our hearts out.

Mum and Dad have been married 28 years and like any marriage, it has had its fair share of ups and downs! But despite the challenges, he has always displayed perseverance and love. Being one of four children, I can imagine that maybe, just maybe, things might have become a little stressful and tiresome for Mum and Dad at times. But they've stuck by all of us through thick and thin. And now that I have been married three years myself, I can appreciate his journey a little more.

One of the greatest things about Dad is his unquestionable love and passion for Jesus. He has been one of the great pillars in my life, pointing me towards a personal relationship with God. I believe he has always tried his best to raise me in the ways of the Lord, teaching me right from wrong and above all to love people. And he's been a great role model to me in the way he fathered—there's never been any area of my life that he wasn't interested in being part of.

Don't get me wrong; no father is perfect. However, as I look back on my life so far, in all the things that truly mattered, my father has been there for me, ready and eager to help me back on my feet. I most certainly and whole-heartedly want to become more like my father! Thank you Dad!

9

Great fathers love their wives

Theodore Hesburgh (1917-2015) was a former president of the University of Notre Dame in Indiana and was one impressive guy. Awarded the Presidential Medal of Freedom (1964) and the US Congressional Gold Medal (2000) for a lifetime of service to his country, he was the recipient of over 150 honorary degrees. Hesburgh served over sixteen presidential appointments for Presidents Eisenhower, Nixon, and Carter. He served on the boards of Harvard University, Chase Manhattan Bank and was Chairman of the Board of the Rockefeller Foundation—one of the world's largest private philanthropic organisations.

To be honest, I didn't know any of that before I did my research. For over twenty years, the only thing I knew about this man was perhaps one of his best-known quotes, which has been included in countless greeting cards and made into posters and wall hangings. He said, "The most important thing a father can do for his children is to love their mother."

Here is a man who has walked with presidents and served his country for the best part of a century and one of the things he's well known for is a greeting card quote exhorting fathers to love their wives.

I find that slightly curious, because Theodore Hesburgh was a Catholic Priest and therefore neither married nor had any children of his own. His quote wasn't something he scribbled down one day to win 'brownie points' with his wife or to explain to his children why he loved their mother so much.

This is pure speculation, but having read about this man, I think the origins of his quote can be found in his years working with disadvantaged groups and dealing with adolescents and young adults at the University where he was president for thirty-five years. I suspect that he saw first-hand the difference that it made to children when their fathers loved their mothers. Notice that he didn't say that loving their mother was just a 'good' or 'helpful' thing to do, he called it "<u>the most important thing</u> a father can do." To paraphrase—above all else, do this!

My Dad's parents were amazing role models. My grandfather, Cyril Thomas Garrett was born in 1895 and served the nation of Australia in both World Wars. In World War I, he fought in the Battle of Messines (as depicted in the 2010 Australian movie *Beneath Hill 60*[6]) and was wounded by a gunshot to the shoulder in France. He built Belrose Church of Christ and devoted much of his life to serving God in that small congregation. Through Grandad's involvement in setting up the local Progress Associations, he was instrumental in having electricity and water connected to that part of Sydney. He was also one of the main instigators to have Mona Vale Hospital built.

However, without doubt, one of Grandad's greatest legacies was his uncompromising love and devotion for his wife of over sixty years—my grandmother. Until the day he died in 1989 at ninety-four years of age, he doted on her. Whenever we sat around the table and talked, he would lovingly hold her hand. He always spoke kind and positive words about the woman he loved and never once did I hear them argue or have a disagreement.

Just over a year after we lost Grandad, Grandma's health quickly deteriorated—she had lost her soul mate of sixty-one years and she passed away soon after, at age eighty-eight.

Having lived with that example, watching his dad love his

mum in that way for more than fifty years, it's little wonder that my dad treats my mum in exactly the same way. They treat each other with respect and always speak kindly about one another.

I've been to a few retirement dinners where the wife speaks about dreading having her husband around the house every day, yet my parents are among the few couples I know who both speak positively about retirement and are excited about spending more time with one another.

In high school, I remember hearing how other kids' parents had separated and were getting divorced. I recall some kids anxiously talking about the poor state of their parents' relationships, and whether they might meet a similar fate.

Disagreements between my parents were rare. Even in the midst of a disagreement, they maintained love and mutual respect for one another, understanding that they were on the same team.

Here's the reason I think Hesburgh regarded his advice to fathers as the most important for their children—because there has never been any doubt that my dad unreservedly loves my mum I have never lived with the insecurity and anxiety that marital disharmony brings.

Never once have I pondered questions like—Will Mum and Dad stay together? If they divorce, would I live with Dad or Mum? If they get a divorce, will I have to move house, move schools and leave my friends? Will we still be able to continue our current standard of living once the family assets are split up? These are questions that no child should have to ponder.

I have watched children who have had to deal with this kind of uncertainty disconnect from the instability of the family, to connect to the more stable friendships around them. When this happens, the parents' ability to have a voice in their child's life begins to diminish.

Without doubt, our best role model is Jesus himself. Through the Apostle Paul in the fifth chapter of Ephesians, God describes His son Jesus as the Bridegroom and the church as His bride. He says that if we want an example of how husbands are to treat their wives, we should follow the example of Christ.

There are some who have difficulty with "Wives, submit yourselves to your own husband as to the Lord" (Eph. 5:22) but I've never met a woman who has a problem with that verse IF their husband is upholding his side of the deal which is found in Ephesians 5:25, "Husbands, love your wives, just as Christ loved the church and gave himself up for her." What woman wouldn't gladly come under the leadership of a godly man who loved her so much that he was willing to give up his life to save his bride?

When my wife and I were engaged, we enrolled in a pre-marriage course at our church. One of the activities we did was to write a statement about our respective roles in the marriage. So I wrote a piece entitled, 'My Role as Cath's Husband.' Here is an extract from what I wrote: *As Cath's husband, I am committed to a life-long partnership with her as my wife. It is my responsibility (and desire) to love her as Christ loved the church…I will always treat her with the highest level of love and respect, and build a lifestyle of serving her, preferring her needs above my own…*

Today, if I were assessed against that goal, would I always score a perfect ten out ten? Of course not, but it's something I strive to achieve every day and with the two generations of role models I've had, that goal is not an unachievable ideal. I have seen it, and to me it's 'normal.'

My prayer is that our three children have the same sense of security that I've known my whole life—knowing that their dad loves their mum, and that also becomes their 'normal.'

Years ago I was working on a project that required me to travel interstate every week for three years. One thing that made the travel bearable was having a regular driver at each end of the journey to avoid lengthy taxi ranks. On the trip home from the airport one Friday evening I asked the driver what he had planned for the weekend. With some excitement, he told me that he and his wife were going on their first date since the birth of their first child. The two of them had not been out on their own for a date in over seven years!

Horrified, I shared the story with my wife, determined not to let their experience become our story. However, we had to concede that we hadn't been as diligent as we should have in prioritising 'us time'; our dates were sporadic at best. With Cath's birthday approaching I bought some beautiful paper from a stationer and designed a voucher book entitled, *12 Dates With the One I Love the Most*. There was an invitation voucher for every month of the year with space for me to complete where we were going, the date and the time. At the end of the twelve months, we had a record of all the dates we'd been on.

It was a simple gift with two very significant benefits. Firstly, it disciplined us to be regular daters in the post-baby phase of our marriage. Secondly, it taught our children that Cath and I prioritised one another. By making a bit of a deal in delivering the invitation each month, even though they were young, the kids learned that quality time for mummy and daddy was something to celebrate.

If you are currently living in a marriage that doesn't look how you want it to, consider Chapter 3, and start to make changes in light of those who are coming after you—your children and your children's children.

If you have been through divorce, this is not intended to make you feel condemned. Rather, I hope that it shows that God's ideal for marriage is possible and even though you might not have experienced that personally or in the marriages of those around you, it gives you something positive and achievable to aim for in the future.

When we marry, many of us promise to love for better, for worse, for richer, for poorer, in sickness and in health, until death separates us. Each of these opposites is meant to describe the two ends of a spectrum; in other words, I will love you when life is going great (that's the better part) and when life stinks (that's the worse part) and everything in between. Yet some people, like the

Skipper (Penguin) in DreamWorks Animation's *Madagascar 2*[7], treat these ends as options.

Acknowledging the uniqueness of the 'relationship' (the Skipper is marrying one of those dash-mounted Hawaiian hoola dolls that bobbles around on a spring), Zuba says, "Love transcends all boundaries. We are here to celebrate such a love. Do you two take each other for better or worse?" to which the Skipper answers, "For better, please."

It's a funny moment in the film, but how many times do we see people in our world making decisions as though they took multiple-choice vows?

I believe that in order to live out the promises we made before God in our wedding vows and to go the distance, there will be times when we need to direct our hearts—not 'follow our hearts.' 'Following your heart' sounds right and terribly romantic, but how many times has this approach brought us grief?

I can think of decisions in the areas of relationships, investments, car purchases, maybe even career choices where I've followed my heart down the wrong path. So many of my car purchases, particularly in my single days, were heart-lead purchases and at times my finances suffered as a result.

The Bible doesn't tell us to follow our heart; we're called to lead it in the way that God says is right. The writer of Proverbs tells us, "Listen, my son, and be wise, and set your heart on the right path" (Prov. 23:19). The reason we shouldn't always follow our hearts is that the Bible says that our hearts can't always be trusted, "The heart is deceitful above all things, and desperately wicked; who can know it?" (Jer. 17:9 NKJV). Your heart can tell you that you don't <u>feel</u> in love with your wife any more, and that's when love becomes a choice, when you remind your heart of the promises you made on your wedding day.

Jesus gave us some good advice to help us locate where our hearts are at, "Wherever your treasure is, there the desires of your heart will also be." (Matt. 6:21 NLT). As we talked about in **Chapter 6 - Great Fathers Make Time**, we can easily find out what is important to a person by looking at where they spend the limited resources of their time and money. If your heart is telling you that you don't feel love for your wife anymore, then what are you treasuring instead of her? Chances are that when you were courting her, you schemed ways to get off work early to spend as much time with her as possible. You didn't think twice about sending that big bunch of red roses to remind her of how much she meant to you and how much you enjoyed the date last night. Now, the new boat, that old car you are restoring, or your newfound love for golf has perhaps become your treasure, because that's where your time and money is going.

If this sounds even vaguely like your life, it's time to take authority and direct your heart. Remind it of the commitments you made, remind it that the next generation is counting on you, watching you, hoping that you will show them how to do relationships well. Then do something practical—start redirecting your treasure back towards the one who was the object of your affections all those years ago.

Great fathers love their wives.

Key Points from this Chapter:

- "The most important thing a father can do for his children is to love their mother." (Theodore Hesburgh)
- Following your heart sounds like good advice for someone who is in touch with their emotions, but the Bible says that the heart can be wicked so we must direct our heart.
- If your heart is telling you that you don't feel love for your wife anymore, then what are you treasuring instead of her?
- To locate where your heart is, look at where you are spending your time and money "For where your treasure is, there your heart will be also" (Matt. 6:21).

MATTHEW'S STORY

I will never forget that day in 1999 when Dad and I drove to a health retreat to pick up my mother. The health retreat staff had called to say they couldn't control or manage her any more. We knew Mum was going to a health retreat with a friend, but we didn't know she had planned to go off her anti-psychotic and anti-depressant medication. By the time we arrived, her friend had gone and Mum was refusing to cooperate with anyone. She eyed Dad and I suspiciously and was obviously having psychotic thoughts. Dad calmly worked for an hour to bring her around, convinced her to come in the car and somehow we made the three-hour drive home.

This is one of many episodes my Dad has encountered throughout thirty years of mum's severe mental illness. Often she would need a hospital stay and always throughout these times, he would visit her. One time, when she had an extended three-month stay in a mental ward, he visited almost every day while working in a high level, well-respected position in the corporate world.

His patience, love, kindness and loyalty towards her is beyond just about anything I have seen in life or read in fiction. He has rarely, if ever, used Mum's illness as an excuse. He is still glad to be alive and remains determined to make the most of every day—in all truth, I'm hard pressed to keep up with him.

Not only has he supported Mum in an incredibly selfless fashion, but he also led our family and raised we three boys. He refused self-pity and would tell us that he didn't want Mum's illness to limit any of us. He did such an amazing job that on occasions when I have told people that my mother has a mental illness, they have often refused to believe me. They struggle to understand how a seemingly successful family can also be carrying someone who required such a high degree of care.

I have never heard anyone say a bad word about my Dad. He treats everyone as a friend and is genuinely interested in them. He'll remember details about people and listen with great intent. At his

70th birthday, his friends told stories about how whenever they go anywhere with him, Dad always runs into someone who knows him!

He also gives generously to our family and to many others. I'm not sure I'll be able to match what I know he has given in my entire lifetime. And yet, I know there is much more he has given that I know nothing about. Reading this, it could easily sound too good to be true, as though I am exaggerating. But the truth is that men like this do exist; men who give even when it hurts and faithfully support their wives, even when their wives can't return the love or partnership to the same level.

Despite the fact that Dad grew up as a Christian and has always taken us to church, that does not automatically make him someone who lives a principled life. I have watched him make good choices, repeatedly, over many years. And I have seen how good those choices are, because they flow into my life and now into the lives of my own children. I also realise how easily and understandably he could have made other choices, given his circumstances.

I have seen firsthand the magnificent fruits of staying faithfully married to one woman, putting others first, refusing self-pity, actively pursuing good friends, committing to a church and putting God first. I'm eternally grateful to my Dad for his example.

10

Great fathers guide, then take a few steps back

As I mentioned, my Dad is the ultimate handyman, he can fix, repair or build anything. In my late teens when I bought my second car, I recall Dad showing me how to carry out basic maintenance like changing the engine oil, removing and checking the spark plugs etcetera. I tried hard. Thankfully, the skin does eventually grow back on your knuckles and God does forgive unsavory language whether verbalised aloud or muttered under one's breath. It would be fair to say that I did not inherit my dad's handyman genes.

Earlier this year, my ten-year-old son and I installed a small, automatic watering system from our rainwater tank to our vegetable garden. A few months later, the water was only randomly spluttering water out of the nozzles. Concluding that the pump on our rainwater tank was about to die I called the pump manufacturer. He said that he was surprised that we'd had ten years of service from the pump, adding that seven years was usually as good as you get. I called an old friend who is a plumber and asked him to drop by and give me a quote to install a new pump. After he left, my wife called me at work to say that the plumber had been and the good news was that there was nothing wrong with the old pump and that it should resume normal operations once we had some water in the tank!

The older I get, the easier it is to have at laugh at my own expense and stories like the water pump have given Dad and I a few good laughs over the years.

Our house is about sixty years old. When we bought it, there was an old air-conditioning unit in the dining area, installed in the space where once there had been a window. I don't think the air-conditioner ever worked since we owned the house, so after we'd been living here five or six years we installed a new split system on the wall above the window. Thankfully, the previous owners had left the original window, accumulating years of dust in the corner of the garage.

At the time we installed the new unit I declared that I would remove the sad old air-conditioner and restore the original window to its rightful place. I doubted my ability to undertake such a task and mentioned to a few friends that I might enlist their help. However around seven years later, over a number of weekends, I stripped the paint off the old window, repainted it and decided to have a go at removing the old air-conditioner on my own.

Within a few hours, I had single-handedly removed the unit and re-installed the window. I was genuinely surprised because it was probably the most adventurous D.I.Y. job that I have ever undertaken on my own. My wife has always been my best encourager and has far greater faith in my D.I.Y. ability than I do, so of course she said how proud she was. I honestly appreciated her affirmation; however, I was keen to find an excuse to call Dad. I thought that he would be as surprised as I was that the job had been completed without a hitch, without blood and without words that needed to be bleeped out.

Dad was less effusive with his encouragement than Cath, but encouraged me nonetheless. Perhaps he didn't think that the job was as out of my league as I did. I must admit that there have been times in my life when I've wondered whether it pains my Dad to see my limited D.I.Y. skills. It's not that he's ever given me any reason to think that, it's purely the pressure that I put on myself because I have this mental soundtrack that says, "Dad wouldn't have called a tradesman for that, he'd have fixed it himself."

One thing that I really appreciate is that Dad has never said, "How about I come over and do that [insert any D.I.Y. task] for you?" which would only convey the message 'I think this one's beyond you.' In every area of life, he has given me freedom to be my own person.

Giving our kids the freedom to develop their own interests, skills and abilities is an important part of parenting. Whilst it's not uncommon for little boys in particular to take an interest in their dad's interests, our goal is not to create little carbon copies of ourselves. If a father is madly passionate about football there is a good chance that his son will be also, and that's great because it gives them a common interest where they can spend quality time together. However, this is not always the case. During our son's season of junior cricket, we saw many passionate cricket dads with young boys who had neither the skills nor the interest in playing the game. As a result, that hour and a half every Saturday morning became a source of frustration in a number of father-son relationships.

The idea of guiding our children and then stepping back is broader than focusing on their natural skills and abilities; it also allows them the space to develop their own interests.

The writer of Proverbs tells us, "Train up a child in the way he should go, and when he is old he will not depart from it." (Prov. 22:6 NKJV). As parents, we are responsible for training our children, providing them with some core skills that will help guide them in life. This verse in Proverbs encourages us to put in the effort to train and teach our children when they are young. As they grow older and our ability to influence them directly diminishes, those foundational life lessons will come to the fore and help them make right choices and wise decisions.

What are some of those areas where we need to train our children? In 1 Thessalonians 5:23, the Apostle Paul encourages us to keep our whole selves blameless and ready for Jesus' return. Just as God is a three part being, Father, Son and Holy Spirit, Paul talks about our three distinct dimensions—body, soul and spirit. So if we are to give our children well-rounded training to prepare them for life, then it makes sense that our training should cover these three dimensions.

The Body is the physical part of a person, and in a very practical sense, we need to teach our children how to look after their physical bodies. They need to have an understanding of the different food groups, healthy eating habits, personal hygiene and exercise. I also believe it is important that we teach them how to cook, not only so they can feed themselves when they eventually leave home, but so they can become contributing members of the family while they're still living at home.

In our early teens, from time to time we were all (including the boys) responsible for cooking a meal for the family. My Mum wanted all of us to transition to adulthood (and marriage) with a broad set of life skills, so we learned to cook, clean and mend our clothes (basics such as sewing on buttons, taking up hems on school trousers etc).

In our many years as pre-marriage counsellors, my wife and I have had some interesting discussions with couples about role expectations within their marriages. During this time we have observed an all-too-common scenario where the young man talks about his mother who has always done everything for him at home. His bride-to-be sits anxiously beside him envisioning their future when they set up home together, feeling the expectation to step into the role of her husband's mother. This inevitably creates tension. At the risk of stating the obvious, we want to avoid any dynamic where one person in a marriage is forced to act more like a parent than a partner.

From a very young age, we have involved our kids in cooking. When our eldest was only two years old, I have some great memories of her at the kitchen table with her apron on, a wooden rolling pin literally as tall as she was, and helping my wife roll out the pasta for ravioli. As they're growing older, the kids each take turns at choosing and preparing dinner a few times during the school holidays (with varying levels of help or supervision).

Puberty can be a challenging phase of life and it is important that we do not leave our children to navigate the 'fog' of puberty on their own. The Bible has a great deal of wisdom around God's design for our sexuality and it is unlikely our children will learn about this at school.

Are we taking responsibility for preparing our children for this phase and coaching them through it, or are we leaving it to the Personal Development teachers at school to teach them all they need to know?

There are plenty of great books to help guide parents through this stage of a child's development. For example, try books such as *Preparing Your Son For Every Man's Battle*[8], and *Every Young Woman's Battle*[9].

God created us to live in community, so look around for other families who are ahead of you in the journey and invite the parents out for coffee. Ask them investigative questions about strategies that worked well with their teenagers, and what things (with the benefit of hindsight) they would do differently.

The other key area of training in the physical realm is teaching our children how to manage money. We live in a materialistic, consumer culture that is obsessed with having the latest, fastest, biggest and best thing. Corporations and advertisers have no hesitation spending billions of dollars each year in an effort to convince us that our lives are incomplete without their product.

Are our actions reinforcing this consumer culture by always

needing to have the latest gadget or trading up to the newest car, even though there is nothing wrong with the two-year-old model we are driving now? Instead, let's set up our children for financial success by teaching and demonstrating to them how to manage a budget and live within their means.

From about age five we have given each of our children a small amount of pocket money each week. Each of them has a moneybox (we use a fishing tackle box) divided into three sections labelled - *Give, Save* and *Live* and we regularly reinforce the purpose of these three categories:

Give – this is what they put in the offering each week in church. We do this because the Bible teaches us in the Old *and* New Testament to 'tithe', which is to give the first ten percent of what we receive.

Save – this portion is for significant future purchases e.g. their first car; it is not for spending on impulse purchases. This is periodically deposited into their bank accounts where they can see it accumulate.

Live – this is for discretionary spending such as school canteen, toys, hiring a movie etcetera. While we try to guide this spending, this is where the real learning takes place. Giving a child the freedom to spend a few dollars impulsively on sweets at the supermarket (knowing it will deplete their spending money for the upcoming family holiday) has to be some of the best value financial education you can give your child.

It is healthy to give your children age-appropriate exposure to some of the financial decisions in the home. For many years we had a small 'fat' television and only a few years ago we decided to buy our first large flat panel television. We were well and truly late adopters—buying our first High Definition TV when the technology had already progressed to the introduction of Ultra HD and curved TVs! We were determined to pay cash, so we saved for about 18 months. We told the kids about this goal, so when we finally brought the new TV home and mounted it on the wall, there was great excitement in the house! We wanted to teach them that it is good to have a goal and save for something that you really want, not just rush out and purchase it with a credit card.

The Soul refers to our mind, will and emotions. We need to teach our kids how to think for themselves, to look at problems and then come up with possible solutions. It is important to introduce them to age-appropriate responsibility. As they get older, they will start to exercise their own free will and make their own choices. If we have made the investment in their younger years—teaching them about making good decisions as well as consequences—when we transition to a less hands-on parenting style, we can be confident that their choices will be based on good foundations.

Helping our children to develop emotional intelligence (EQ) is a key life skill. EQ is a measure of how well a person relates to others, how aware they are of their own emotions and how their emotions affect those around them. From the time they started school, when our children have made sweeping emotional statements such as 'I'm angry' we've tried to encourage them to think about and verbalise the feelings behind the anger. Too often 'anger' is a convenient catchall, when the real emotion is frustration, disappointment, exasperation, annoyance, impatience or some other negative feeling. At work, in marriage and in friendships, emotionally healthy adults need to be able to identify and articulate different emotions in themselves and in others.

It is also our responsibility as parents to teach our children how to develop good friendships and how to be a good friend.

At times when our children have come home from school and relayed stories about 'friends' not behaving as friends should, we use these opportunities to teach our children about what good friendship looks like. Asking your child, "How do you think a good friend would have reacted in that situation?" turns the situation into a learning experience instead of telling them to simply, "Stay away from Johnny."

When we are over-protective and too quick to jump in to rescue a child from a testing relationship, we lose the opportunity to teach them how to do life alongside difficult people. I am not suggesting that we leave a child in a dangerous or abusive relationship. However, learning to deal with difficult people in life is an important skill. We might be able to request that the school shift our child to a different class to avoid another child or even perhaps a teacher who they do not get along with, but what happens when they enter the workforce and their first boss or colleague is not the easiest person to get along with? It's better to invest the time in building key relationship skills when our children our young.

The Spirit is the life that God breathed into us when we were created. The Bible teaches us that a person's spirit is influenced either by the spirit of the world or the Spirit of God (1 Cor. 2:11-16). The spirit of a person knows the thoughts, will and actions of the person. When a person surrenders their life to God, their spirit enters a relationship with God himself through His Holy Spirit who then lives within them.

In terms of training our children spiritually, it is our role as parents to teach them that we are spiritual beings. I think that many people believe this to be true even if they do not believe in God, however, for Christians, the most amazing truth is that we can have a relationship with our Heavenly Father, the one who created the universe and everything in it; the one who exists outside of time, the natural realm, and all that we can see with our natural eyes.

Not only should we teach our children about God from His written Word, but also through the quiet witness of how we live our lives—through our actions and decisions. After observing the lives of my parents and my paternal grandparents, the evidence for me was clear. The blessing and favor, the comfort, strength and hope in tough times, all led me to the conclusion a long time ago that I wanted to pursue my own personal relationship with God.

Another key area where we need to learn to exercise this principle of 'guide and stand back' is in the area of careers. I have seen fathers place extraordinary expectations on their children to follow a particular career path or groom them to take over the family business, and it rarely ends well. Either the child rebels and does their own thing or complies and leads a miserable, unfulfilled life.

Having worked as the Head of Human Resources for a bank, I saw this played out all too often. Typically, branch managers would call to say they were having performance issues with a particular staff member. By the time they involved me, the person would have had two unsatisfactory performance reviews, and the call from the manager was to inform me that they had notified the individual that if they received a third unsatisfactory review, they would be dismissed. It was at that point that I would get involved with the dismissal paperwork and potentially, with union officials.

Obviously, it's not a pleasant process and so one time I thought I'd short-circuit the process. I requested the manager send the staff member (let's call him Mark) to my office. Mark sat waiting in reception, slumped down and staring at the ground; his body language clearly conveyed that he was expecting the worst. I invited him into my office and instead of sitting behind my big desk, I sat around on the other side of the desk with him. I spoke first.

"Hi Mark, thanks for coming to see me at such short notice. I understand that you and your manager haven't exactly been having the best time at work lately."

"No" said Mark, his eyes still staring at the carpet.

"It seems to me that nobody is winning in this working relationship. I don't know if you enjoy the work you do, but you're obviously not happy at work and as a consequence that's making things miserable for those around you—your manager and colleagues. Tell me, do you actually enjoy the work you do?"

"Not really." he responded, stating the obvious.

"Tell me a little bit about why you chose a career in banking." I asked.

"Well…" he started, finally making eye contact, perhaps responding to the fact that someone was seeking to understand him as a person "…when I left school I was a little unsure of what I wanted to do. My dad told me that banking was a secure profession so he thought I should get a job in banking."

"Now, with the benefit of being a little older and having some life experience under your belt, if you could choose to do anything you want, what would you do?"

Without much hesitation he said, "I've always wanted to get into acting."

"With all due respect to your dad, he's not the one that's turning up to the bank five days a week, forty eight weeks a year, being miserable. It's your life and life's too short to spend the next thirty years doing something you hate. What's stopping you from following your dreams and having a crack at acting?"

Mark didn't answer the question, but his facial response was like a light bulb had been switched on inside his head, as if he'd realised that his dad's career advice, no matter how well meaning, had become like a jail sentence. Maybe it was the reality of over thirty years of continuing the charade, just to keep his dad happy, that confronted him.

I didn't ask him for his resignation, I simply thanked Mark for his time and for being so openly candid with me.

"Well?" my assistant asked as Mark disappeared from view behind the lift doors, "Did he resign?"

"No," I said, "I didn't ask him to."

The next morning, after sorting the mail, my assistant came into my office with a stunned look on her face, waving a letter in her hand; it was Mark's resignation.

That story was re-enacted time and again, only the name of the staff member changed. In fact, it happened with such frequency that my assistant asked me what went on in my office that resulted in staff resignations inevitably arriving in the mail shortly after meeting with me.

The 'secret' is simple—people are not made to live each day with the pressure of trying to live up to someone else's expectations, or the consequent antagonistic relationships with colleagues and the boss. When someone in a position of authority takes a personal interest in them, seeking to understand the dreams and desires buried within them and respectfully informs them that no-one else should hijack their happiness, they feel released to take responsibility for their own future and act accordingly.

One of the aspects of God's character that I find remarkable is that He created us with free will—the ability to choose—fully aware that many will use that freedom and choose to turn away from him.

We read in Genesis 1:7 that God created us in His own image. When I read this, I imagine the process of God making the first man—Adam…

…He puts in each of his own characteristics (a bit like plugging individual fuses into a giant fuse board)—love, kindness, creativity and so on. Then he selects 'free will/choice,' and for a moment, He hesitates before deciding to plug it in. Because He sees the beginning from the end, He knows how this is going to end… 'If I give them free will, some will use it to choose NOT to have a relationship with me.' And yet He gives it to us anyway, because He knows that a relationship without choice is not relationship at all.

We could learn a thing or two from our Heavenly Father in this regard. We have fourteen or so years to train our children and then we gradually begin to step back, allowing them to slowly assume personal responsibility for their life and become their own person. If we lay strong foundations when our children are young, we can have the same confidence that Abraham showed in Genesis chapter 13, when he and Lot went their separate ways.

Abraham says to his nephew Lot, "Is not the whole land before you? Let's part company. If you go to the left, I'll go to the right; if you go to the right, I'll go to the left." (Gen. 13:9)

Abraham understood that God's presence and blessing was not limited to only one of these choices; he was confident that God would be with him, regardless of the direction he went.

So when it comes to career choices, it can be detrimental to impose our opinions upon our children. Maybe you are trying to steer your children towards a high-paying career so they won't have to struggle financially. Perhaps you're trying to pressure them to follow in your footsteps because your chosen career has afforded you great opportunities and lifestyle. But why not encourage your children to follow their own dreams? Pray for God to bless them with fulfillment, favor and influence, whichever path they choose. As King Solomon wrote in Ecclesiastes, "So I decided there is nothing better than to enjoy food and drink and to find satisfaction in work. Then I realised that these pleasures are from the hand of God." (Eccl. 2:24 NLT)

I thank God that my father never placed expectations on me about career, about who and when to marry, or where to live. He never made me feel inadequate for calling a plumber or for taking my car to the mechanic to have the oil changed. He put in the hard work when I was young and watched me become my own man. When we try to remove the issue of choice from our children, we do something that even God himself wasn't prepared to do.

Great fathers guide their children in the things of God and then at the right time, they take a few steps back and watch them become their own person.

Key Points from this Chapter:

- Our role as fathers is to invest the time in training our children when they are young.
- Our children need core life skills that address body, soul and spirit.
- Give your children the space to develop their own skills and interests.
- Having put in the time when they are young, we should equip them as adolescents with the skills to transition to adulthood. Over time, our relationship with our children becomes less like a teacher and more like a coach as they take on greater responsibility.
- The wisest man ever—King Solomon—said that there is nothing better than finding satisfaction in your work. Avoid placing your own career expectations on your kids; instead encourage them to find a career where they will find satisfaction.

PETER'S STORY

As an only child of unskilled migrant parents, my father worked hard to establish a footprint in this country and provide for his family the best way he could. Financial pressures were always present, but his sense of humour, love of life and fun, (even if it made my mother cranky), created a bond and treasure bank of memories. Dad was my father and best mate.

Dad was our provider, in every way. From the basics of food and shelter, he also completed domestic chores, cooked for the family, played cards and joked around. We had fun. Dad would have the occasional 'flutter' on a horse race if he knew it was a sure thing, and the winnings would pay for a takeaway dinner on a Saturday night.

We went to church most Sundays and he would sing in a falsetto voice or a bass so low I couldn't help but laugh, often at my mother's displeasure who would position herself between us. He didn't go to the pub, or hang around with his mates after work. He loved my mother.

Dad died thirteen years ago and I miss him every day. Would I change the way he raised me? Not a chance. He instilled a valuable work ethic in me to provide for my family in every way, create many memories, keep a sense of humour and to love my wife.

While growing up, I must have been subconsciously watching my father because without setting out to do so, I can see that I have repeated my father's ways with my 6 children and perhaps added in a little faith as well. I fall well short of being a perfect father, perhaps too quick sometimes to over provide, or a little slow knowing when to let go. When I asked my middle (teenage) daughter how I was doing as a father, she said that she wished that I were more demonstrative in showing fatherly affection. It was great feedback because on reflection I can see that I withdrew in that area as she entered her teenage years.

If I want to keep growing as a dad, I need to be prepared to accept critique from my wife and children and say sorry if I'm in the wrong. If I can't do this, how can I expect my children to change when I ask it of them?

My wife and I have always had the perspective that we are not raising children; we are raising young adults, and as such have tried to treat them with respect and give them age appropriate responsibilities. But let's see what my oldest son has to say ...

NATHANIEL'S STORY:

I hear a lot of guys in my world say that they don't want to be like their dads, but that's not me; my dad has been a great role model.

Through his example, my father has taught me a lot about life, including the importance of hard work, how to deal with different types of people, and how to love my family. He showed me what it means to be a man, and most importantly, how to become my own man.

Dad taught me to make my own life and to fight for what I believe in. He has always encouraged me to follow my dreams and make my own decisions, but regardless of which path I chose, he was always there if I needed anything.

For example, Dad has always enjoyed helping us with our assignments and revision at school. However, when it comes to technology, Dad will be the first to admit he's no guru. So when I chose to study IT at university, I knew it would change his role as my study mentor because I was venturing into unfamiliar territory for him. Nonetheless, he understood that it was something I was really interested in, and accepting that his role would change, he urged me to follow my interests.

When I was younger, I would often go surfing with Dad. It wasn't just the surfing; we both enjoyed the time talking in the car as we drove to and from the beach. When I started hanging out with my friends more and getting to bed later, the 4:30am starts to join Dad surfing just didn't happen. I know Dad missed spending that time together, but he never forced me to come along when I was tired.

Our relationship continues to change as we transition through different phases of life, and at times I think that's meant some uncertainty for Dad as he wonders what our roles will look like in the next phase. But despite this, he's never tried to hold me back or influence my direction.

So while I haven't set out to become a copy of him, I know that as I follow in Dad's footsteps, I will inevitably become more like him, and that's a good thing. Without him, I wouldn't be the man I am today.

11

Great fathers give and receive respect

Choose any sphere of life—sports, politics or the arts—and you can probably think of people who have made a significant contribution to their particular discipline. However, whilst you may respect the specific contribution they have made, you may not necessarily respect the actual person.

Perhaps it's a sportsman who has scored more goals than anyone in the history of the game, and for that reason you respect their achievement. Off the sports field, their life could be a total wreck and therefore it's difficult to respect them outside of their achievement.

Therein lays the peculiar nature of respect. We can respect a particular individual's skills and abilities, without necessarily respecting the person as a whole.

Dictionary.com describes respect as *esteem for or a sense of the worth or excellence of a person, a personal quality or ability, or something considered as a manifestation of a personal quality or ability.*

The type of respect I am referring to goes way beyond respect for a single ability or quality. For example, I respect his money management skills, or I respect how he balances his time between work and his family. The respect found in great fathers is a holistic respect; it speaks of a deep regard, an all-encompassing and unqualified honor and reverence for the person as a whole. That is why I positioned this chapter last—I don't think there is one single quality or characteristic to focus on in order to be respected. The father who loves his wife, shows grace, takes responsibility, leads consistently etcetera, will earn the respect of his wife, his children and those around him, not just because he instructs his children to 'respect me because I'm your father.'

Around the middle of the first century AD there was a young Greek man called Timothy who became the leader of the early church in a place called Ephesus (modern day Turkey). He had previously been on a few missionary trips with the Apostle Paul and helped him in his work. In 1 Timothy 3, Paul is writing to Timothy with some fatherly advice to his young protégé regarding the selection of leaders in the church. He lists a number of characteristics to look for: The leader should be well thought of, love his wife, show self-control, live wisely and have a good reputation. He must not be a heavy drinker or be violent. He must be gentle, peace-loving and not a lover of money. "He must manage his own family well and see that his children obey him, and he must do so in a manner worthy of full respect." (1 Tim. 3:4)

The context of this passage is church leadership, but notice the characteristics that qualified a person for leadership in the church had little to do with their activities within the church. Paul did not say to look for someone who is a great teacher, good at counseling and pastoral care, or someone who has great charisma and can lead worship. Instead, it was a man's success in leading his family, his good character and standing within the community that qualified him to be a leader in the church. So the church leadership criteria essentially describe how to be a great father, whether we choose to be involved in church leadership positions or not.

In light of Paul's checklist to Timothy, when I look at the lives of my two great fatherhood role models—my grandfather and my dad—they each score ten out of ten. Their conduct in leading their own families and their standing within their respective communities is what qualified them for leadership within God's house.

The Bible talks about having a deep reverence and respect for our Heavenly Father. It is often referred to as the 'fear of God.' In fact, there are over three-hundred New and Old Testament references to fearing God. Proverbs 9:10 says, "The fear of the Lord is the beginning of wisdom, and the knowledge of the Holy One is understanding." So if we want wisdom, it starts with fearing God.

Exodus 18 reveals how fearing God is a prerequisite for leadership. Moses' father-in-law comes to visit and gives his son-in-law some timely advice. He tells Moses that his current workload of single-handedly governing the Israelites is not sustainable and that he's heading for a breakdown.

In his wisdom, Moses heeds his father-in-law's advice and delegates his workload to appointed leaders. One of the key selection criteria when Moses was recruiting these leaders was their fear of God.

"But select capable men from all the people—**men who fear God**, trustworthy men who hate dishonest gain—and appoint them as officials over thousands, hundreds, fifties and tens." (Ex. 18:21)

Let's be clear: when talking about the fear of God, the Bible isn't saying that we're to be scared of God. Dictionary.com lists a number of different meanings for the word 'fear.' One example is *a distressing emotion aroused by impending danger, evil, pain*; obviously that's not what the Bible is talking about. The other explanation is *reverential awe, especially toward God: the fear of God*.

In contrast, when we reduce our understanding of God to that of a loveable Santa Claus figure onto whose lap we climb to ask for stuff, we will neither fear nor respect Him. However, when we have a revelation of the awesomeness of Almighty God as the one who formed the universe with the creative power of His words, and when we understand His power and majesty (Job 42:1-2; Rev. 4:11) we can then understand why God is to be feared. The recognition that God need only utter a word and I could cease to exist, causes my worship of Him to be out of reverential awe for His utter and immeasurable power.

In God, we see the unique combination of fear and love in that, with all His awesome power God desires a relationship with you and me. He chooses not to deal with us as our sinful nature deserves, instead, He shows us grace and mercy.

As fathers, we can earn the respect of our children by the life we lead and the decisions we make. To receive respect, we also need to give respect. Do we model respect to those in authority— for example, those in government and law enforcement?

Whenever I hear parents speak poorly about the Police, I look at their relationship with their children and often I observe children who are disrespectful towards their parents. It is an inescapable truth that we reap what we sow. Do your children see you sowing respect?

Another characteristic that will cause your family to respect you is to know that you fear God. Is your reverence and awe of him something that is evident in the way you live? Or do the decisions you make demonstrate a greater fear of man? When your teenager asks if their girlfriend or boyfriend can sleep over (and I don't mean sleeping downstairs on their own in the guestroom), do we give a God-honouring answer or are we more afraid of what our child's friend (and his or her parents) might think if we say no? Perhaps we are more afraid of what our own child might think of us if we say no.

Given the choice between living with the fear of what my children and their friends may think of me versus the fear of God, I would rather live in the fear of God by respecting and obeying him. But remember, it is a choice.

Great fathers live a life worthy of respect. When they fear

God, show respect to others and make great choices across every area of life, they will naturally earn the respect of others.

Key Points from this Chapter:

- The respect that can be found in (and for) great fathers is a holistic respect; it speaks of a deep regard, an all-encompassing and unqualified honor and reverence for the person as a whole.
- To receive respect, we also need to give respect. Do we model respect to those in authority—for example, those in government and law enforcement?
- Is our reverence and awe of God something that is evident in the way we live, or do our decisions demonstrate a greater fear of man?
- Not only does the Bible say that the fear of the Lord is the beginning of wisdom, in several instances it lists fearing God as a prerequisite for leadership.
- In the early church, the prerequisite for becoming a leader was to be respected by your family and those in your community.

BEN'S STORY

The one thing that everyone has in common is that we are all someone's child.

As the oldest of four kids, I guess my journey with my father had an average start. However, I hope my story shows that significant change is possible, and that something great can emerge from ordinary beginnings...

One of the biggest blessings in the early years of my life was that I always felt safe when I was with my dad. I still remember one particular night when I was about six years old when my dad took me for a walk. I recall feeling a real sense of adventure rising on the inside of me as we walked into the pitch-black night. Dad was teaching me about the speed of light, and the enormity of the universe. Looking up at the stars, I admired my father's knowledge; I felt loved and respected because he chose to share his knowledge of the universe with me.

As we were walking along, we stopped in the middle of a field next to our house. Dad pulled out a torch. Asking me to hold it with him, we pointed the torch into the sky and he said, "Let's send a light beam into the sky TOGETHER." I can still hear him explaining to me how this beam of light would continue to travel throughout the entire span of our lives. (Twenty years down the track, I wonder where in the universe that beam is now.)

What was so special to me was how Dad involved me in everything he did. He taught me so many things—useful life skills that I use every day. The time I spent learning from him was so precious.

Dad has always been a good provider; in a material sense, I have never had to worry. However, in my teenage years, I was also seeking emotional support from him, yet we never really developed a trust-based relationship. Through most of those years, I struggled with very low self-esteem and a fear of failure. Discouragement was my constant companion. My father was never abusive, but he would become really angry if I accidentally broke something or made a mistake. But when I did something well, I cannot recall ever receiving a single word of encouragement or the affirmation that I was desperately looking for. I was convinced I was a failure and that I wasn't good at anything. This led to a deeply discouraged heart, which significantly influenced some choices I now deeply regret.

A real turning point came when I was seventeen, my parents decided to embark on a journey that changed our family forever. They both enrolled in Bible College in Australia and so our family moved from Langenschiltach in Germany to Sydney, Australia.

I have such high respect for Dad as I have watched him grow immensely in his fatherhood over the past nine years—the direct result of that one decision. I don't know of another dad who has grown as much as he has in this amount of time.

My parents have since completed their studies and returned to Germany with the rest of my family. I have remained in Sydney to complete a Master's degree in Theology. This has only been possible because of the constant encouragement and financial support that my dad has given me over the last five years. He has sacrificed so much, caring for the well-being of our family. Each of us are now flourishing in what we do; a testimony to my father's wisdom, faithfulness, consistency and his commitment to personal development. He loves God, has loved my mum through every season, invests himself into building the local Church, and is also currently building his own business.

In recent years, I've gained some valuable insight into the family circumstances in which my dad grew up. As a child, he did not receive the respect and encouragement he needed from his father, so it is little wonder that he was unable to give it to me. Considering this, I admire how he has overcome many of his personal struggles and discouraging circumstances.

Because of his choices, he is even more of a hero to our family today than in the past. His constant support and his selflessness are key traits that have helped me to build the trusting relationship with him that I was longing for in my teens; it has also helped me to forgive him for the mistakes of the past. Today, more than ever, I love him and respect him as a father and a true friend!

12

A final word

What an amazing honor and privilege it is to be a father...
and what a responsibility! Fatherhood goes way beyond
playing our biological part in the creation of another human life.
Not only do we help shape that new life, but with a generational
perspective, we are also shaping the lives within the life.

Regardless of your experience with your own father, you can
choose the type of father you want to be; however, unless you
make a conscious choice, chances are you will become a repeat
of your father. For some that is a good thing, but statistics tell us
that all too often it is not the case.

The cool thing is that if you identify any great characteristics
that you lack as a dad, you can start right now to make a change.
Perhaps you need to make some changes to your work schedule
to reprioritise time with your kids, or maybe your relationship
with your wife has become a little too transactional. Within you
is the ability to learn new skills and habits such as the ones covered
in this book.

It is always interesting to me when a guy says, "Yes, but you
don't understand, I've never been good at setting boundaries with
my time." I like to challenge that kind of thinking. There was a
time when none of us knew how to drive. There is hardly a man
alive who didn't count down the months until they could get

their learners' permit, even studying the road rules in advance to pass the learner's test and be ready for their first driving lesson. The point is, we are prepared to go to extraordinary lengths to acquire new skills and abilities if we place value on the benefits that those skills bring. The freedom and autonomy that a driver's license brings means we'll do whatever it takes to pass the test.

So in terms of your motivation to change, what type of father do you want to be? My guess is that if you are reading a book about the characteristics of great fathers—the type of fathers whose children love and respect them so much that they want to become more like them—then 'average' is not for you.

My sincere hope is that you are not even satisfied with just being a 'good father.' Sure it's better than being mediocre or average, but don't our children and their children deserve better?

My prayer is that regardless of your upbringing, you are inspired to be a great father, a man who goes way beyond the minimal requirements. I hope you're like a magnet to your children's friends, so that on Friday nights or the weekend when they're choosing whose house they want to hang at, they choose your house because they know you always take an interest in their world. They know that at your place, you will be consistent and always have an encouraging or affirming word. They know there will not be any awkward moments between you and your wife because you always speak lovingly and respectfully to each other.

Imagine inspiring those young men to be the type of husband and father they want to become one day, and the young women to have hope in their hearts, determined to aim high and not just settle for the first boy who shows an interest in them.

Importantly, our children's relationship with (and view of) their Heavenly Father will be largely influenced by their experience with their earthly father. If we discipline out of love instead of anger, separating the behaviour from the individual (i.e. that behaviour was bad vs. you are a bad child) then scriptures about the Lord's discipline will make sense to them and they will be less likely to withdraw from God when they've sinned.

"My child, don't reject the Lord's discipline, and don't be upset when he corrects you.

For the Lord corrects those he loves, just as a father corrects a child in whom he delights." (Prov. 3:11-12 NLT)

Similarly, accepting God's grace becomes easier when earthly fathers have modeled grace to their children when they make mistakes.

We are not designed to do this journey of fatherhood alone. Firstly, we need to be in relationship with God our Heavenly Father. The Bible is full of great wisdom, and if we develop and cultivate our relationship with the Holy Spirit, He will prompt us and guide us as we lead our families.

Find at least a few good, godly men in your world with whom you are sharing the journey. I was disturbed to read some recent research[10] that found one quarter (or 1.1 million) of Australian men in the 30-65 year age category have few or no social connections and around a third of these men were not satisfied with the quality of their relationships. Sadly, just over three quarters of men said that they did not feel emotionally supported and did not think that their mates could help them with the problems they were facing.

American entrepreneur Jim Rohn said, "You are the average of the five people you spend the most time with." That is a very interesting and perhaps sobering thought. Look at the handful of people you hang with the most and ask yourself whether you are comfortable with being the average of them. Do you need to re-prioritize some friendships when it comes to time in your diary?

We all need to find some good men with whom to walk the fatherhood journey; men who care about us enough and have permission to speak into our lives if we start making poor choices that will sabotage our future. Look for men whose lives demonstrate the characteristics described in this book and learn from one another.

Proverbs 27:17 advises, "As iron sharpens iron, so one person sharpens another."

"Walk with the wise and become wise, for a companion of fools suffers harm." (Prov. 13:20)

As you begin growing in wisdom and become respected as a great dad, look for opportunities to invest into other men. As you mentor those coming after you, you will become an inter-generational influencer as you influence the people within the people.

"Train up a child in the way he should go, and when he is old he will not depart from it." (Prov. 22:6 NKJV)

My personal prayer is that there be nothing about my life that becomes an obstacle when it comes to my children's relationship with God as their Heavenly Father. I am training them in the things of God and I trust His Word—that when they are old they will not depart from it. When God reveals different aspects of His character to them, I trust that they will recognize (and not struggle with) that part of His nature because they saw it role modeled by their earthly father. I want to be their biggest cheerleader, to encourage them and set them up for their own amazing adventure in life.

Will you join me in becoming more like The Father?

STEVE'S STORY

Dad was one of nine children. He was mostly raised by his older brothers as his father died when he was only nine years old, leaving his mum to raise them all on a widow's pension. Although he didn't get to finish school, he developed a strong work ethic through working first for a newspaper company, followed by becoming a machinist and then learning the trade of a skilled carpenter builder. Later on, Dad went to Bible College. Since then he has devoted his life to serving God in various ways, including pioneering and pastoring churches, running a Bible college and as a missionary for over a decade in Papua New Guinea (PNG), where I was born.

I love my dad and I know he loves us—Mum, my three sisters, our spouses, children and grandchildren. Although he is not perfect and has his particular quirks, Dad has always been a genuine, honest, passionate and hard-working man who cares about his family, friends and faith—all to which he has given his best.

A carpenter by trade, it seems Dad has always been building or fixing something. As I was growing up, we shared a special connection as he included me in his projects, patiently teaching me all he knew about his tools and working with timber. I have such fond memories of him helping me to build things. He built me a large table under our house for an electric train set with papier-mâché mountains and tunnels. Later in high school, together we built a large aviary in which I kept and bred parrots. For my wedding day, Dad blew me away when he made an entire suite of furniture, including our bed and dining table. Since that day, that table has been the place where my own family has shared countless meals and many joys and challenges.

When I was about six, I can remember walking into our family dining room one particular day where Dad and Mum sat chatting over a usual cup of tea. As I left the room, something triggered in my heart as I reflected upon how much they loved to talk about Jesus and helping people. Since that day, Dad and Mum have continued to live selflessly and tirelessly for others, showing us that purpose is found in living for something bigger than yourself, like the cause of the Kingdom of God.

Dad isn't tall in stature, but to me, he stands tall in character. Over many years, he has led us through some amazing adventures—the stories could fill a book. The early years of my life in PNG included trying to cross flooded rivers, contending with snakes and crocodiles, traversing muddy, slippery roads and keeping our jeep from sliding over the edge of a cliff! On occasions when one of us faced a life-threatening sickness, like the time my sister had dysentery, we saw Dad seek God for healing. There was no hospital or doctor for miles, but Dad prayed and we saw God heal her.

Growing up in Australia, Christmas holidays were such a highlight for me. Dad bought a caravan and we had wonderful adventures exploring much of eastern Australia. I also loved travelling with dad when he would go to speak at churches. My world enlarged as I encountered so many different ethnic churches. Even the simple things, like grabbing McDonalds on the way home, were part of these special times with dad.

Dad wasn't a rich man, but I consider him among the wealthiest fathers I know and I wouldn't trade my heritage for anything. Dad's wealth has been in his life experience, his faith and in how generously he has lived for others. At home, there was always room at our table for people to share a meal or a bed if anyone needed a place to stay. I'm convinced we unknowingly witnessed the miracle of feeding many with our version of the five loaves and two fish.

When it came to church and his faith, Dad has given his life to pray in secret, to preach in public and serve with grace and humility. Only Heaven will reveal the thousands of lives his ministry has forever touched. To this day, in the village where he now lives, Dad continues to help those in need and lead people to Christ.

My dad is my hero.

Acknowledgements

Firstly I want to thank my amazing wife, Cath. I am so blessed to do life with you. Because of your constant encouragement and continued belief in me, this book was written. Thanks for the countless hours you've invested in this book, correcting my grammar and improving my writing even before it went to the editor.

To our three wonderful children—Madisson, Thomas and Joshua—being your dad is one of the greatest joys and privileges of my life. Because of you, I'm committed to doing whatever it takes to be the best dad that I can possibly be.

Thanks to my parents. I know at times you thought I had unrealistically high expectations for finding a wife, but you guys set the bar incredibly high in terms of marriage and family and I was determined to settle for nothing less. Thanks also for allowing me to share our story.

Thank you to my siblings whose personal stories have been shared in this book.

Thanks to Ruth for editing the book, for your expertise, continual encouragement and guiding me through the writing process.

Thanks to Nicole and Belinda for encouraging me and sharing your wisdom and years of experience as authors.

For many years the unfinished manuscript sat buried on my laptop. Thanks to Linda who heard from God and took a risk in saying to me—a virtual stranger—'God told me to tell you, it's time to finish the book.' At the time, you had no idea what it meant, but I did. I thank you for being a faithful messenger.

Finally, thanks to our amazing pastors for constantly encouraging us to live others-focused, large, open and expansive lives (2 Cor 6:11-13 MSG).

References

1   *I Am Not My Father*, Paul Scanlon © Paul Scanlon 2007, Abundant
    Life Publishing, Wapping Road, Bradford, West Yorkshire BD3
    0EQ, ISBN: 13 978-0-9555804-1-3
2   *The Battle For the Loins*, Paul Scanlon, © Paul Scanlon 2004, Abundant
    Life Publishing, Wapping Road, Bradford, West Yorkshire BD3
    0EQ, ISBN: 0-9538516-1-3
3   *Taking Responsibility For Your Life*, Pastor Andy Stanley North Point
    Community Church, Atlanta, Georgia, http://yourmove.is
4   *Fathers spend seven times more with their children than in the 1970s,* The
    Guardian, Sunday 15 June 2014, article written by Tracy McVeigh
    and Isabel Finch http://www.theguardian.com/lifeandstyle/2014/
    jun/15/fathers-spend-more-time-with-children-than-in-1970s
5   *The Queen of Versailles*, documentary film by Lauren Greenfield,
    Magnolia Pictures, Evergreen Pictures
6   *Beneath Hill 60*, Paramount Pictures, released 2010
7   *Madagascar 2*, DreamWorks Animation, released 2008
8   *Preparing Your Son for Every Man's Battle*, Stephen Arterburn, Fred
    Stoeker with Mike Yorkey, © 2003, 2010 Stephen Arterburn,
    Fred Stoeker, and Mike Yorkey, Waterbrook Press, ISBN:
    978-0-307-45856-8
9   *Every Young Woman's Battle*, Shannon Ethridge, Stephen Arterburn,
    Waterbrook Press, ISBN: 978-0-307-45800-1
10 *Men's Social Connectedness*, Beyond Blue research funded by the
    Movember Foundation, Hall & Partners Open Mind report June
    2014, Vicki Arbes, Charlie Coulton and Catherine Boekel

Printed in the United States
By Bookmasters